After Christendom

Michael Warren Davis

AFTER CHRISTENDOM

SOPHIA INSTITUTE PRESS
Manchester, New Hampshire

Sophia Institute Press
Box 5284, Manchester, NH 03108
1-800-888-9344
www.SophiaInstitute.com

Sophia Institute Press® is a registered trademark of Sophia Institute.

hardcover ISBN 978-1-64413-760-4
ebook ISBN 978-1-64413-761-1

Library of Congress Control Number: 2024936653

First printing

For Rod Dreher,
who opened my eyes

Only the hand that erases can write the true thing.

—Meister Eckhart

Contents

Acknowledgments

FIRST AND FOREMOST, I would like to thank Tim Stanley. In 2022, Tim reviewed my first book, *The Reactionary Mind*, for the journal *Modern Age*. His review was extremely generous and full of terrific insights. One of those insights, however, hit me like a thunderbolt:

> Davis is right to castigate moderns for suggesting everything today is better than yesterday, but I struggle with the claim that most of yesterday was better than today. And if you peel back his fustiness, what the author is really arguing for is a greater commitment to the teachings of Jesus Christ, which in their own day were regarded as revolutionary. Were he a Roman in the 1st century, would Davis, like a good traditionalist, light his garden path with burning apostles? Or would he, as I suspect, embrace the newfangled ideas of the bearded Judean, i.e., that women have rights and slaves are equal to their master?

I'm afraid Tim was wrong. I could easily see myself having sided with the Romans and the Pharisees against Jesus, flea-bitten reactionary that I am. But I want Tim to be right about me—and his review caused me to do a great deal of soul-searching. *After Christendom* is the result. So—cheers, Tim.

My thanks also to Andrew Oliver, for putting this book into shape, which was a Herculean effort. Really, he deserves a co-author credit.

To Steve Dawson and Chris Check for their invaluable insights about street evangelism and apologetics.

To Kevin Knight, for graciously permitting me to use New Advent's editions of the *Didache* and the *Letter to Diognetus* as appendices.

Most of all, I would like to thank my wife and daughters, whom I neglected terribly while finishing this manuscript. I'm awed and humbled by your patience, love, and support. I'll never be able to repay the debt I owe you, though I'm looking forward to making up for lost time. I love you more than you'll ever know.

Introduction

Mystics, Martyrs,
and Missionaries

---

*The Lord knows the reasonings of man,
that they are emptiness.*

—Psalm 93:11

Progress is the scourge God has chosen for us.

—Nicolás Gómez Dávila

I believe that we are living through the greatest catastrophe since the fall of Rome. Western civilization is dead. Christendom is no more. What we see around us now isn't Christian; it's not even a civilization. It's a mummified corpse—and even the wrapping bands are beginning to fray.

Of course, the West could be reanimated someday. It died once already, to its old pagan self. Then it rose again in the Middle Ages, made young in the Faith. It may rise once more. But if it does—and that's a big *if*—it will look very little like it does today. Why? Because there's so little worth salvaging.

Remember: politicians, journalists, and think-tankers have a vested interest in our believing that victory is imminent, or at least possible. The populist Right likes to talk about "Zombie Reaganism" and its "dead consensus," but this is only a way of disguising its own failures. The conservative elite will blame this or that faction for the Right's failure to resist the Left, but, in reality, it is the Right that has failed. It exists now only as a vast Ponzi scheme to enrich those politicians and journalists and think-tankers, who then use their wealth and power to insulate themselves from the consequences.

We have no need for "conservatives." There is very little left to conserve. In any case, it wasn't conservatives who resurrected the West or saved the West from decadence and anarchy. It wasn't liberals, or socialists, or centrists. It wasn't businessmen or lawyers or emperors or kings or queens.

No, it was mystics, martyrs, and missionaries. They must save the West again.

That's my thesis in a nutshell. In this book, we'll look at just how bad the situation has become and how much worse it's going to get. Then we'll discuss how Christians can survive, even flourish, in the coming Dark Age.

I believe that we *will* flourish. I believe that, once again, the tears of the mystics, the sweat of the missionaries, and the blood of the martyrs will become the seed of the Church.

Believe it or not, this is a hopeful book. We're in the middle of a great drama, the greatest since the Resurrection.

Two thousand years ago, the Church conquered the world. But the Church divided against herself, first in 1054 and again in 1517, and fell into five centuries of heresy, apostasy, revolution, and dissipation.

True, in some countries, such as the United States, Christians are still a numerical majority. But *believers* are already a small and hated minority. Everywhere in the Western world, those who cling to the orthodox Faith are reviled—by their rulers, their neighbors, even their own shepherds.

But if hope has finally run out, and the end looks near—and all is lost—suddenly, a still, small voice; and the beating of wings ...

1

The Final Christian Generation

And they sacrificed their sons and daughters to the demons,
and they poured out innocent blood, their sons' and daughters',
blood, in sacrifice to Canaan's idols, the land sick with
murdered blood, the land polluted with these deeds.

—Psalm 105:37–39

I will have no praying-men to put a fear
of death into men's hearts.

—H. Rider Haggard

When folks talk about the end of Western civilization, usually they're talking about the paraphernalia: art, music, literature, architecture, politics, economics, and so forth. By the way, I don't call it "paraphernalia" to put it down. All of that stuff deserves to be mourned, and I mourn it.

But I agree with Christopher Dawson, who asked, back in the 1920's, "whether men are happier or wiser or better than they were in simpler states of society, and whether Birmingham or Chicago is to be preferred to Medieval Florence." Are things, culturally speaking, any better today?

William Butler Yeats was onto something, and most of us know it:

> Things fall apart; the centre cannot hold;
> Mere anarchy is loosed upon the world,
> The blood-dimmed tide is loosed, and everywhere
> The ceremony of innocence is drowned;
> The best lack all conviction, while the worst
> Are full of passionate intensity.

Deep down in our bones, we feel this is true. But who let loose the blood-dimmed tide? When did everything start to go wrong? I have a theory.

During the Wars of Religion (1552–1648), Europe's Catholics and Protestants slaughtered each other by the tens of thousands; violence-driven disease and famine claimed the lives of millions more. Europe was exhausted, both physically and spiritually. In the late 1600s, the West's finest minds rallied together to blame those wars on religion itself. They set out to build a new political, cultural, and intellectual order based solely on reason and natural law. We call this project the Enlightenment.

It failed. And it failed for the most honorable reason: it was too Christian. Its champions (quite literally) couldn't imagine a world without Christianity.

Put it this way. Pretend you've never heard of Christianity. Purge your mind of all of Jesus's teachings. Now think of a few good deeds that you think any rational person would recognize as good.

Odds are you thought of something like "Giving money to a homeless person" or "Volunteering at a soup kitchen." Surely, you thought, helping the poor and needy is a safe bet.

Wrong.

In his masterpiece *Dominion*, Tom Holland talks about how Julian the Apostate, the last pagan emperor of Rome, wrote a letter to the priests of Cybele complaining that they were failing in their duty to care for the poor. As Holland points out, Julian's letter would have baffled its readers. The cult of Cybele was completely monstrous and had no interest in the poor.

You see, Julian was raised Christian—and it sounds as if he paid attention in Sunday school too. Because really, not just the Cybeles but any true pagan would have balked at his letter. None of antiquity's great philosophers ranked compassion very high on the list of virtues. In fact, many of them considered empathy a vice. "The strong do as they wish," said Thucydides, "and the weak suffer what they must."

In fact, as David Bentley Hart points out in *Atheist Delusions*, the cornerstone of Nietzsche's philosophy is his belief that Christianity brought about a "slave revolt" in Western values, "a new and sickly *moral* vision of reality, judging all things, noble or base, according to the same pernicious and vindictive categories of good and evil." Aristotle and Plato, Cicero and Seneca all took for granted the moral right of elites to enslave and abuse the weak, the stupid, and the poor.

Really, we have no idea what it means to be "post-Christian." Like Julian, we have no idea how many of our most fundamental moral assumptions are grounded in the Christian religion. And it is very difficult to imagine what the world will look like when those foundations crumble.

Take another example. Pro-life advocates often accuse the pro-choice crowd of being "anti-science." After all, biologists have definitively proved that life begins at conception. These activists believe that if only they can get liberals to "believe the science," liberals will see the error of their ways and abortion will be banned forever.

Actually, the opposite is going to happen. Eventually, those liberals are going to say: "All right, fine. Life begins at conception. But who cares? It's just a bunch of cells. Let's just go ahead and kill it anyway."

"By that logic," the pro-lifer will respond, "a newborn is just a larger 'clump of cells.' The act of being born doesn't magically change a fetus into a baby."

"Hey, you're right," they'll say. "It *is* basically the same thing. I think a mother should be able to kill her baby, too, if she doesn't want it anymore."

You don't believe me, dear reader. I don't blame you. But it's true: abortion and infanticide are, and have been, commonplace in every non-Christian society. Scipio was the exception; Hannibal was the rule.

From at least the 1600s until the last century, most rural Japanese families committed infanticide as a matter of course. The practice was known as *mabiki*, or "thinning out"—the same word farmers used for the purging of smaller plants from an overcrowded field. Once a father felt he had more children than he could afford to feed, he might smother his newborn. It was common for poorer families to kill two or three children this way.

Japanese infanticide was unusual because it was mostly boys who were killed. Most cultures have preferred to snuff out their girls. In the Icelandic saga of *Gunnlaugur the Serpent-Tongue*, a husband named Thorstein tells his wife, Jogfridr: "So you are with child. If you shall bear a girl, it shall be exposed, but if a boy, it shall be raised."

Thorstein sounds a lot like Hilarion, a certain first-century Greek businessman. All we know about Hilarion comes from a letter he wrote to his pregnant wife. He wrote: "If it is a boy, keep it. If it is a girl, discard it." Lovely. But he was no anomaly. Most ancient Greeks took the same attitude toward child-rearing. So did the Romans. They were particularly callous toward feeble offspring. "Unnatural progeny we destroy," Seneca explained; "we drown even children who at birth are weak or abnormal."

Nor was Hilarion an anomaly among civilized, middle-class Hellenics. As Rodney Stark has observed,

> Seneca regarded the drowning of children at birth as both reasonable and commonplace. Tacitus charged that the Jewish teaching that it is "a deadly sin to kill an unwanted child" was but another of their "sinister and revolting practices." ... Both Plato and Aristotle recommended

infanticide as legitimate state policy. The Twelve Tablets—the earliest known Roman legal code, written about 450 BCE—permitted a father to expose any female infant and any deformed or weak male infant.

When Christians today talk about infanticide, we usually think of demon-worshippers like the Carthaginians or the Aztecs, diabolists sacrificing their children to their demonic gods. And we mustn't forget these dreadful rites, especially now that Satanists are demanding their First Amendment right to perform "ritual abortions." Yet, as G. K. Chesterton points out, these demon-worshippers pay a perverse honor to children. They seem to know what babies are worth. They sacrifice their young precisely *because* they see their worth. They're like Abraham, before the angel stayed his hand.

But the Spartan attitude is far more common. They took their weak children deep into the woods, where their screams couldn't be heard, and left them to be eaten by wild animals.

Even today, the Chinese commit infanticide on an industrial scale. Really, female infanticide is a pillar of Chinese culture. Journalists blame the practice on the Communist Party's "one-child policy," but that's only a small part of it. Chinese parents have been murdering baby girls for thousands of years, a form of *mabiki* meant to conserve resources for male children, who can help their fathers in the fields. Female infanticide is still widely practiced in China's rural provinces, with tacit approval from the Communist Party.

This is what a non-Christian society looks like. It's what the West looked like before the advent of Christianity; it's what the West will look like soon, once the last vestiges of Christendom have been stripped away. Mothers and fathers will kill their newborn babies simply as a matter of convenience. And they'll feel no shame. None whatsoever.

It's not just the babies, either: the elderly, the sick, the deformed, the poor ... Outside of Christendom, their lives have always been disposable, and they will be once again, here in the West. Mark my words. We'll snuff out their lives without a second thought.

You don't believe me, dear reader. You can't imagine your mothers and fathers, your sisters and brothers, your friends, committing such evil deeds. I don't blame you. But imagine going back in time a hundred years. Imagine trying to explain modern politics to your great-great-grandmother:

> Every woman has the right to abort her pregnancy up to the moment of birth, and old people can end their own lives through physician-assisted suicide. Even if the old people don't want to kill themselves, sometimes doctors will do it anyway. Doctors will also kill you if you have cancer ... or depression, or autism.... Just ask. Oh, they'll also cut off a little boy's gonads if he wants. And the boy's parents can go to jail if they try to stop him.

If you could have told anyone in the 1920s that *this* is what America would look like in a hundred years, they would have called you mad. If you'd said their own great-grandchildren would be the ones urging these doctors to kill babies, murder old people, and mutilate children's genitals, they would have biffed you right in the eye. It's offensive! It's disgusting! It's unthinkable! But it's true.

Name a single vice that was popular in the late Roman Empire, and you'll see that it's already making a comeback in the twenty-first-century West. Slavery? Our economy is powered by slaves in countries such as China and Pakistan. That was the whole point of outsourcing. Pederasty? After normalizing transgenderism, the Left's intellectual vanguard is preparing to do the same for "minor-attracted persons," or MAPs. Scholars, psychiatrists, and legislators are already demanding that the age of consent be lowered dramatically so that adults can legally have sex with children. Blood sports? Rioting, looting, assault, and murder are now common in our major cities. At first, we pretended they were political protests; but for many, this is a form of recreational violence, and the government does nothing to stop it. No one really cares.

Most alarming is the return of paganism. For the most part, conservative Christians believe the West is drifting toward atheism. I wish that were the case. The void left by Christianity will not remain empty for long. Witchcraft, sorcery, and Satanism will rush in to fill the vacuum. Even today, woodlands across the country are being used by covens of witches and diabolists. I've witnessed it myself. God help me, I've taken part in those rituals. This is the world we live in now.

As bad as things seem now, they will be infinitely worse in a century or two. Ours is not the most perverse or degraded society in human history. It's not even close. And remember, that perversity has nothing to do with whether a society is civilized or not.

Saint Basil speaks of orgies in which men eat until they vomit and then begin the next course; they eat until they vomit again; the next course is served—over and over again, until the sun begins to rise. This, mind you, is very much an upper-class pastime. You have to imagine the hedonist discussing Thales or reciting Horace while gorging themselves; then he toddles home, past all the wailing newborns who've been left on the sidewalk to die, before sodomizing the ten-year-old boy he bought at the slave market that morning. Then it's a quick trip to the bathhouse before watching the Christians burned or devoured by panthers in the Coliseum.

This was the greatest civilization the world has ever seen.

Yes, things could get much worse. And they will. Mark my words: in a hundred years or so, *your* great-grandchildren will be the ones murdering their own babies, having sex with children, casting spells on their enemies, and killing poor people for fun.

That may seem like disgusting slander. It *is* disgusting. But it's not slander. I'm tempted to say, "It won't be their fault," because in a sense they won't know any better. This kind of behavior is all too normal in non-Christian civilizations.

Study after study shows that, within a generation—and for the first time in seventeen centuries—Christians will be a minority here in the West. This is our not-too-distant future.

Either you get that, or you don't. And if you don't, you're part of the problem. I'm sorry to be the one to tell you. I'm sure you'd like to help. But, look, when the *Titanic* has struck an iceberg, and half the ship is underwater, if you are trying to figure out where to get supper once we dock in New York, you're not helping.

There isn't going to be any supper tonight, my friends.

This is why we must not idolize political or ideological movements and think they are going to save us. That goes for the Left, of course. But it also goes for the Right: conservatism, populism, Christian nationalism, integralism—the lot. It doesn't matter how clever their schemes for the future may be: if they don't take into account the total collapse of Western civilization, they're essentially useless.

In fact, they can be worse than useless, if they ply us with false hopes. False hopes are servants of the Enemy. They're his fifth column, which he plants deep within our own hearts and minds. They lull us into a false sense of security. They make us lazy, complacent. Then, when he's ready to attack, they throw open the gates.

Throughout the rest of this book, I'll be suggesting ways to prepare for the coming Dark Age. But I'll consider my job well done if I can sell you on just one point: the Dark Age *is* coming. More likely than not, it's already here.

2

Despise the World

Human salvation is emptiness.

—Psalm 59:11

Christ is our Liberator insofar as He is our Savior.

—Augustine of Hippo

"What gives you the right to say that Christendom is dead?"
you may be asking. "Our fathers in the Faith won the
West for Christ. They consecrated our whole society to
God. They belong to Him, and so do we. We're *His* people. We
have no choice but to defend *His* nations from *His* enemies."

Men and women who take this position have got the proper
fighting spirit. But, with Saint Augustine as my witness, I say that
they're wrong.

When you are pondering the death of civilization, Augustine is
the one man you can't do without. Though he is best known today
for his spiritual memoir, *The Confessions*, Augustine's greatest con-
tribution to Christian thought is his tome *The City of God*, which
he wrote as a direct response to the sack of Rome in A.D. 410.

The Eternal City fell to the Visigoths just thirty years after
Theodosius declared Christianity the official religion of the Roman
Empire. The Romans themselves were, understandably, baffled.
How could God have forsaken them so quickly? Maybe the pagans
were right after all. Maybe they should repent and turn back to
Jupiter and Juno and Minerva ... As the saying goes, "Drought
and Christianity go hand in hand."

Augustine's answer to these doubts has thundered across history, and echoes Saint Paul. "For there is no power but of God,"
the Apostle wrote; "the powers that be are ordained of God." Or,

as Augustine put it: "God, who gives happiness in the kingdom of heaven to the pious alone, gives kingly power on earth both to the pious and the impious, as it may please Him, whose good pleasure is always just."

Now, Paul and Augustine aren't saying that we should blindly obey whoever happens to be in power. Clearly, they could distinguish between good and bad rulers, between just and unjust laws. Their point is simply that God can use both good and bad rulers to accomplish His will.

Of course, we can learn this by reading the Old Testament. Over and over, the Israelites abandon God. Over and over, God allows Israel to be humiliated by idolaters—first, the Egyptians, then the Babylonians, then the Romans. Why? Because He knows that, in their distress, the Israelites will turn back to Him.

This is Augustine's whole point in *The City of God*. The Father is taking power away from Christians and giving it to pagans. By depriving us of this worldly good, He fosters in us a greater *spiritual* good: repentance. Christ will gladly allow the City of Man to burn to the ground if, by doing so, He helps us turn our hearts back to the City of God.

Augustine isn't afraid to push his thesis to its logical conclusion, either:

> Lest any emperor should become a Christian in order to merit the happiness of Constantine, when every one should be a Christian for the sake of eternal life, God took away Jovian far sooner than Julian, and permitted that Gratian should be slain by the sword of a tyrant.

Just so we're clear, Augustine is arguing that God granted Julian the Apostate the long reign that he used to dismantle the Roman Church. Why? So that no future emperor would embrace

Christianity for the wrong reason. He allowed the Magnus Maximus to assassinate Gratian so that good politicians wouldn't make presumptions on His favor.

In short, says the Doctor of Grace, "earthly kingdoms are given by Him to both the good and the bad; lest His worshippers, still under the conduct of a very weak mind, should covet these gifts from Him as some great things."

Once again, Augustine doesn't deny that good government is ... well, *good*. He denies that it's *great*. When we have it, we should be grateful for it. When we can, we should strive for it. But it is a luxury that we should be able to live without. The Master made that much abundantly clear. "And ye shall be hated of all men for my name's sake," Christ warned, "but he that endureth to the end shall be saved."

Persecution, not power, is the norm for Christians. It always has been. It always will be.

Western Christians are emerging from a long epoch of power, and it feels unnatural, even wrong. It feels like power should be the norm. And, looking back at the glories of Christendom, we wonder how God could want anything less for His people. But maybe that's why God allowed Christendom to fall.

The question is: *What are we going to do about it now?* Here, too, we should look to Saint Augustine.

It's the feast of Saint Cyprian, in the year of Our Lord 405. The sack of Rome is still five years away, but the Empire is now in a state of terminal decadence. Augustine is addressing his congregation in Hippo Regius, one of the great centers of Roman Africa. Most of the flock is, like Augustine himself, a mix of Latin and Berber. But they can see the writing on the wall: if, or, rather, *when*, the Eternal City falls, she'll drag the whole empire down with her.

The Christians of Hippo were asking the same question we're asking now. *How should Christians live in a post-Christian West?* Augustine's answer is simple. Look to the Early Church. "Despise the world, Christians," he cries, and then, again:

> Despise the world. Despise it. The martyrs despised it. The apostles despised it. The blessed Cyprian despised it, whose memory we are celebrating today. You all want to be rich, want to be held in honor, want to enjoy good health; the man in whose memory you have come together despised the lot. Why, I want to know, do you have so much love for what the man you honor like this had such contempt, the man whom you wouldn't be honoring like this if he hadn't held it all in contempt? Why do I find you to be a lover of these very things whose scorner you venerate? Certainly, if he had loved these things, you wouldn't be venerating him.

Like the old prophets, Augustine calls the Romans to repentance—and he stresses that our repentance must be individual as well as corporate. We must take personal responsibility for Christendom's death. God isn't punishing "us": He's punishing you. He's punishing me.

And so, Augustine continues,

> You all say, "The times are troubled, the times are hard, the times are wretched." Live good lives, and you will change the times, and then you'll have nothing to grumble about.... Who was ever harmed by the rising of the sun, who was ever harmed by its setting? So time, then, has never harmed anybody. It's people who are harmed, and people whom they are harmed by.

Order and anarchy, justice and injustice, sin and repentance: either we do them, each of us, in our turn, or they don't get done at all.

To be clear, I'm fully aware that anyone who credits any current event to "God's judgment" will immediately be dismissed as a fundamentalist, a sandwich-boarder, and so forth. I don't mind. In modern parlance, a *fundamentalist* is just someone who believes the unpopular bits of Christianity.

And for believers, this is really all just common sense.

Even in the Old Testament, God doesn't actually *punish* the Israelites. Remember, Israel is a little fish in a big pond. It is always the underdog. Whenever the Israelites defeat an enemy, whether it's the Amalekites or the Egyptians, the Canaanites or the Romans, they need God's help.

When the Israelites turn away from God, they're simply refusing that help. When they fall into idolatry, they're rejecting His favor. They know where their meals come from, so to speak, and yet they freely choose Ba'al over Yahweh. Saint James says, "Every good gift and every perfect gift is from above, and cometh down from the Father of lights." We have nothing good apart from God. We can't reject Him without rejecting His blessings. Or, as C.S. Lewis put it: "God cannot give us a happiness and peace apart from Himself, because it is not there. There is no such thing."

The West flourished when it served God. The West suffers because it has rejected God. The West will flourish again when it repents and turns back to God. What could be simpler?

Before we move on, though, I want to stress two things:

First, I don't cite Augustine because he's the greatest theologian in the history of the Latin Church (though he *is* that). I cite him because he was the chief architect of Western Christendom's first renaissance. By following his lead, our fathers in the Faith were able to survive the fall of Rome. And not only did they survive, but they forged the greatest civilization humanity has ever known.

Secondly, I'm not a historian or a theologian or a political philosopher. I'm not here to define the ideal Christian society or anything of the sort. I'm just here to make a few suggestions as to how we—as Christian individuals, families, and communities—can respond to the crisis of the early twenty-first century.

I do believe, however, that this crisis has arisen because we Christians have failed to take personal responsibility for the Church's apostolic mission. For too long, we've ignored the Master's command to preach the Gospel to all nations, to "go into all the world and preach the gospel to every creature." For too long, we've outsourced that witness—to the State, to the institutional Church, to our neighbors. And, to be sure, all have a role to play.

But we need a new strategy. Or, rather, a very old one. We need to follow the example of Augustine and Cyprian, of Peter and Paul.

The Lord is calling us, each by name: "You also go into the vineyard."

So, let's be off.

3

Two Masters

The Lord said to my Lord, "Sit at my right hand
until I make thine enemies thy footstool."

—Psalm 109:1

The Lord would rather wash the feet of
His weary brothers, than be the one perfect
monarch that ever reigned in the world.

—George MacDonald

ugustine's message can be summed up pretty well in the word *xenitia*. It's a word you hear quite a bit in the Greek Fathers. It means "otherness" or "foreignness." The *xenitemenos* is a man far from his homeland. For the Greeks, particuarly Saint John Climacos, xenitia is often regarded as the first step in the spiritual life: we must develop a deep awareness that this earth is not our true home.[1] We're resident aliens in the City of Man; our place is in the Kingdom of God. The Christian must take James Bond's motto as his own. *Orbis non sufficit*: "the world is not enough."

Tragically, most Western Christians have lost their sense of xenitia. We don't feel estranged from this world. We don't *want* to feel estranged from this world.

This is readily apparent in the Church's progressive wing. To a large extent, their religion is merely a kind of "spiritualization" of left-wing politics. Whenever they speak about their faith (if it can be called faith), it is clear they take their cues more from the *New York Times* than from the New Testament. They carry on about how the Church ought to focus on combating climate change or marrying same-sex couples or ordaining women — not exactly the

---

[1]   Xenitia is related closely to nostalgia, whose root words are also Greek: *nostos* (return) and *algos* (pain). Xenitia is the agony of exile; nostalgia is a longing for home.

concerns of historical Christianity. Much of what they desire is, in fact, positively heretical. But that doesn't bother them. They don't mind butting heads with God as long as they're on good terms with Mammon.

It isn't only the liberals, however. The Church's conservative wing is also infected with worldliness, albeit in a much subtler form.

For instance, Pope Leo XIII wrote ninety encyclicals—nearly a third of all the papal circulars issued to date—many of which pertained to politics (rather than political issues). Up to that point, the Church had been reluctant to adopt "official" positions on social and economic issues. Leo, however, was the first pope in more than a thousand years to wield no political power: in 1870, under the reign of his predecessor Pius IX, the Kingdom of Italy finally absorbed the last vestiges of the papal states.

Unable to pass laws of his own, Leo attempted to exercise "soft" power by issuing dozens of encyclicals on statecraft and economics, most famously his *Rerum Novarum*. From that point on—and for the first time in the history of the Catholic Church—popes began attempting to forge an official Catholic political ideology. The Vatican also encouraged the formation of Catholic Action groups to spread its ideology.

About twenty years after Leo's death, Pope Pius XI issued his encyclical *Quas Primas*, which established the Feast of Christ the King. Pius made it clear that the new feast was a direct response to the decline of the Church's earthly power. "As long as individuals and states refused to submit to the rule of our Savior," Pius wrote, "there would be no really hopeful prospect of a lasting peace among nations."

While the title "Christ the King" is an ancient one, it became hugely important to Catholic counterrevolutionary movements, from the French royalists to the Mexican Cristeros. In other words, the Feast of Christ the King is a permanent sign of the Church's refusal to accept the postrevolutionary order. It is Rome's attempt to remind us of its own political authority. Even if the Holy See is unable to rule directly, it still feels entitled to hand down the principles by which governments and economies ought to be run.

Different popes, of course, have brought different emphases to their social teachings. John Paul II focused on fighting Communist totalitarianism; Francis pays more attention to immigration and environmental policies. The point is that, at an institutional—and perhaps even a *doctrinal*—level, the Catholic Church firmly believes in her own secular, as well as religious, authority.

Despite the challenges posed by the current pontiff, a belief in the Church's secular authority is built into the DNA of the "Catholic Right." And this is true not only of more radical groups such as integralists; it goes for more generic conservatives as well. From William F. Buckley to Pat Buchanan to Marco Rubio, Catholic conservatives have often appeared to seem duty-bound to defend Christian—or at least "Judeo-Christian"—civilization.

But, as we saw in the previous chapter, this conservative instinct (broadly speaking) violates the most basic tenets of Christianity. Regardless of whether the papal magisterium extends to politics and economics, all power in Heaven and on Earth belongs to God. Even the Roman Church is not *entitled* to authority; Christians do not *deserve* to wield power.[2] Roman Catholic apologists, or "conservatives," who imply that they do are not just foolish; they are borderline heretical.

[2] Of course, this is not an attack upon the Catholic Church. Regardless of what some ideologues might claim, Rome does not dogmatically claim a right to political power.

But laying claim to power—even if it is done only in the abstract, and power itself never realized—makes it almost impossible for us to become *xenitemenoi*. And, again, xenitia is the very first stage of spiritual development. The Lord says, "But seek ye first the kingdom of God, and his righteousness; and all these things shall be added unto you"—the "things" being food, water, and so on. In other words, we're not supposed to become saints *while also* trying to achieve social justice (or the common good, or whatever you want to call it). We're supposed to devote ourselves to becoming saints and let God add the rest.[3]

Usually, you can tell when a Christian rejects xenitia by the way he talks about the Roman Empire. For instance, Sohrab Ahmari—a leading member of the integralist clique, and a good friend of mine—published a review in *First Things* of *The Church of Apostles and Martyrs* by Henri Daniel-Rops, which had just been republished by Cluny Media. Sohrab saw Daniel-Rops as a kind of forerunner to the integralist (or "Political Catholic") movement:

> "The Revolution of the Cross," as the author calls the rise
> of Christianity, pitted a new doctrine against the ideology
> of an established imperial order. Sadistic madmen like Nero
> aside, some pagan rulers recognized this fundamental op-
> position and proved to be the most ferocious and systematic
> of the early Church's persecutors. And yet, just as there was a
> providential synthesis between Greek philosophy and Judeo-
> Christian revelation in the realm of ideas, so there was a
> natural kinship between the legal and political practice of
> Rome and that of the nascent Church. The result was that,

---

[3] Before anyone starts: no, this isn't "quietism." This is what Lewis meant by aiming for Heaven and getting Earth thrown in.

notwithstanding the violence meted out by Rome to Christians, the Church came to assume Roman political forms. For Daniel-Rops, the essence of this unlikely congruity is *universalism*, beginning with Rome's drive to subject all nations to its own governing rationality. The Romans built reliable roads linking their vast domains. And down these roads they spread the same legally ordered way of being in the world, whether their subject peoples liked it or not.

Broadly speaking, it's true that the Church became enmeshed with the State over the first four centuries of the Christian era—and, broadly speaking, that's a good thing. In fact, I think that Saint Constantine is the greatest gift God has given to mankind since Pentecost.

Yet there are genuinely *Christian* reasons to push back on Daniel-Rops's thesis. Because, while Church and State often worked well together, they just as often … well, *didn't*. As Philip Sherrard pointed out, "Christianity spread for three centuries not with the state, but in spite of it, not in conquest but in the catacombs."

Even in the early 600s, Saint Gregory the Great felt the need to remind Europe's rulers that "humility and kindness, teaching and persuasion, are the means by which to gather in the foes of the Christian faith."

In 772, Charlemagne implemented a policy of forcibly baptizing the Saxons. When they resisted, he sent his armies into Saxony with orders to burn their crops. This went on for years and years, with the Franks slowly starving the Germans for refusing to accept Christ. But Charlemagne's chief adviser, Saint Alcuin of York, openly and loudly dissented from his master's policy. "Let people newly brought to Christ be nourished in a mild manner, as infants are given milk," he said, "for instruct them brutally and the risk then, their minds being weak, is that they vomit everything up."

As Tom Holland recounts in *Dominion*, Charlemagne and Alcuin liked to argue about religion or politics while enjoying a hot bath together. In the course of one such soak, Alcuin won Charlemagne over. Eventually, the king rescinded his policy of forced conversion in Saxony.

To be clear, neither Alcuin nor Gregory believed the Germans had a "right" to be pagan. They did not. They weren't proto-liberals. They simply opposed forced Christianization, on both ethical and practical grounds.

Likewise, we have the example of Saint Boniface. He famously cut down an oak tree that was believed to be sacred to the god Thor (or maybe Odin; the record isn't clear) and used the wood to build a church. That's how he lived. The story of how he died, however, is not as well known.

Just as the sun was dawning on June 5, 754, Boniface and his company were attacked by a band of Saxon pirates. The Christians drew their swords—all except their leader, Boniface, who ordered his companions to lay theirs down. They had come to preach the Gospel, not to shed blood, innocent or otherwise. His companions did as he asked and, as they knelt to pray, the missionaries were hacked to ribbons.

Boniface hated heathenry, but he loved the heathen. He knew that nothing mattered but the conversion of sinners. He also knew that nothing could convert sinners except the living God. He gave up everything he had for that mission, including his own life. But he used the proceeds to win Germany for Christ.

That's why Saint Boniface, not Charlemagne, is known as the "Apostle to the Germans." The emperor put his trust in the Empire; the saint put his trust in God.

So it is true (as my good friend says) that the Romans used their roads to "spread the same legally ordered way of being in the world."

And it's true that, often enough, Christian rulers used their governments' infrastructure to spread the Christian faith, "whether their subject peoples liked it or not." But, as the saints make clear, this is not a fulfillment of the Christian ideal. It is a *betrayal* of the Christian ideal. For Christianity is nothing more than the love of God, who is Himself love. One man can't force another to love God any more than he can force another to love *him*. That's not love at all. It's rape.

There are Roman Catholics who go deeper, arguing that *Romanitas* ("Roman-ness") is, in fact, a theological principle. Alan Fimister, who is the co-author of a book on integralism and the author of *The Iron Sceptre of the Son of Man: Romanitas as a Note of the Church*, defends exactly this point of view.

Early in his book on *Romanitas*, Professor Fimister invokes a famous passage from Hilaire Belloc's *Europe and the Faith*:

> The history of European civilization is the history of a certain political institution which united and expressed Europe, and was governed from Rome. This institution was informed at its very origin by the growing influence of a certain definite and organized religion: this religion it ultimately accepted and, finally, was merged in. The institution—having accepted the religion, having made of that religion its official expression, and having breathed that religion in through every part until it became the spirit of the whole—was slowly modified, spiritually illumined and physically degraded by age. But it did not die. It was revived by the religion which had become its new soul. It re-arose and still lives.
>
> This institution was first known among men as RES PUBLICA; we call it today "The Roman Empire." The Religion which informed and saved it was then called, still is called, and will always be called "The Catholic Church."

It is worth noting that Professor Fmister does not quote the final sentence of this passage from Belloc, where Old Thunder declares: "Europe is the Church, and the Church is Europe." This, of course, is the logical conclusion of everything Belloc has said. It's also complete nonsense.

Jesus was a Galilean Jew. All of the first bishops, the Apostles, were ethnically Jewish. The first known foreign convert was an Ethiopian. The name "Christian" was coined in the Greek city of Antioch, in modern-day Turkey. The first country to adopt Christianity as its official religion was Armenia.

For the first three hundred years, Romans are the great *antagonists* of the Christian Church. Yes, they do help the Faith to spread—but only by killing their Christian citizens *en masse*. For, as Tertullian says, "The blood of the martyrs is the seed of the Church." If the Roman elite had had their way, however, the Jesus Cult would have died with Jesus.

What's more, several Roman pontiffs—including Leo XIII, Benedict XVI, and John Paul II—have declared dogmatically that the Eastern (i.e., non-Roman) churches possess the fullness of the Faith. The latter explicitly spoke of "the divinely revealed and undivided heritage of the universal Church which is preserved and grows in the life of the Churches of the East as in those of the West." In other words, the Church is no more essentially "Roman" than it is essentially Galilean, or Ethiopian or Antiochian or Armenian.

It is perhaps understandable that Belloc made this mistake in 1920. In his own time, there was less contact between the Christian Occident and the Christian Orient. But how could anyone hold this opinion in 2024? Why do so many intelligent, faithful Catholics believe that the living Church is somehow bound up with the long-dead Roman Empire, which Constantine virtually abandoned in favor of his eponymous city, and less than twenty years after legalizing Christianity? Why don't they at least follow the Orthodox in identifying the Church with the Byzantine Empire, and the New Rome in Constantinople?

Any serious scholar or theologian of any creed will admit that the identification of the Church with "Old Rome"—the Latin Empire—has no basis in the Early Church. In fact, it was a political device used by Frankish and German princes who tried to establish themselves as the legitimate heirs of the Western Empire by aligning themselves with the Patriarch of Rome against the Byzantine emperor (i.e., the legitimate Roman emperor).

This is all ancient history, of course. But even by the internal logic of *Romanitas*, there's nothing essentially Roman—or Latin—about the Church. A medieval Franco-German heresy has somehow become orthodoxy among traditionalist Catholics.

Why are so many folks so keen to insist on the "Roman-ness" of the Universal Church? I think that's clear enough. It has nothing to do with history or theology or ecclesiology. It's all politics. As Daniel-Rops makes clear, Rome is the universal symbol of power in the Western world. This is true for us just as it was for Belloc—and Charlemagne. Whoever identifies himself as Caesar's heir identifies himself as the locus of legal, economic, military, cultural, and (yes) religious authority. If we can "prove" that the Christian Church is the successor to the Roman Empire, perhaps we can also claim the loyalty of Western civilization.

But this is a fool's errand. TikTok trends notwithstanding, modern Westerners don't care about the Empire any more than they do about the Church. This is all cope, a massive campaign to trick ourselves into believing that Christendom is just one tweet away from being restored to its former glory.

To put it another way, conservative Catholics are trying to find a way of being Christian without practicing xenitia. Like liberal Catholics, they want to practice their Faith while keeping the peace with our elites. The only difference is that conservatives want to swap in a more favorable class of elites.

Ultimately, though, very few conservative or liberal Catholics are willing to accept the world's hatred, which was promised to us by Christ. Both are reluctant to suffer for their Christian beliefs. (And I don't blame them! Honestly, I don't.)

And of course, this problem is not limited to Catholics. You can easily find the same malaise among Protestants. Listen to the way they talk about the Founding Fathers' religious beliefs, and you quickly realize that they, too, feel entitled to power.

Truth be told, I'm not sure how many of these conservatives will stand with the Church when she once again finds herself a small, poor, despised minority sect. Many young right-wingers are abandoning the Faith already, going over to neopagan movements such as the alt-right. (And it's hard to blame them either.)

So much of our identity as "conservative" Christians lies in the Church's worldly power. We perceive ourselves as the heirs of Rome, the *silent* majority, the *moral* majority—the once and future kings of Western civilization. Well, now the Church's membership is collapsing. Her political and cultural influence has dried up. For many on the Right, this discredits the whole Christian project. Christianity, as defined by conservatives, has failed.

The good news is that conservatism isn't the same as Christianity. Not at all.

The answer is not to define ourselves for or against our "post-Christian society." In a way, there's no such thing as society, as Margaret Thatcher observed. There are only *men*—men choked by despair and dying of sin who can be saved only by the love of

God. This is true in twenty-first-century America no less than in twelfth-century France or second-century Rome.[4]

The only truly "common good" is Jesus Christ. The only way to Heaven is through His Divine Person. Nothing else matters. It never has. It never will.

Remember that the Pharisees rejected our Master precisely because He refused to destroy their political opponents. And they had good reason! They had been told that, when he came, the Messiah would be a great warrior-king. He was supposed to drive the Romans from the Promised Land. Instead, He was arrested and crucified.

Even those who knew Him best, such as Peter, refused to believe that He could die at the Romans' hands. And once He was dead and buried, what did the apostles do? They sat around in the upper room, dazed and confused. No matter how many times He predicted His own death, they wouldn't—they couldn't—believe Him.

We may not realize it, but so many of us today commit the exact same sin as the Pharisees. We believe that our God must be a conquering God. We would sacrifice the pure teachings of Christ on the altar of political power. We reject the role of suffering servant. We refuse the cross.

---

[4] For any gender-neutral word police that are disquieted, Margaret Thatcher was also fond of quoting Winston Churchill's observation: "Grammarians will attest that Man embraces woman, unless otherwise stated in the text."

4

Culture War or Great Commission?

Who is the man who desires life, who loves to behold good days? Keep your tongue from evil and your lips from speaking deceit. Depart from evil and do good; seek peace and pursue it.

—Psalm 33:12–14

It is only with the heart that one can see rightly.

—Antoine de Saint-Exupéry

Before we go any further, I should probably concede that little I say here is especially original.

I myself first came across these ideas in Charles Péguy, who wrote:

> It is the mystic who is practical, and the politically minded who are not. It is we who are practical, who do something, and it is they who are not, who do nothing. It is we who accumulate and they who squander. It is we who build, lay foundations, and they who demolish. It is we who nourish, and they who are parasites. It is we who make things and men, people and races. It is they who wreck ruin.

C. S. Lewis made the same point in his masterpiece *Mere Christianity*. In chapter 10 ("Hope"), he warns that,

> If you read history you will find that the Christians who did most for the present world were just those who thought most of the next. The Apostles themselves, who set on foot the conversion of the Roman Empire, the great men who built up the Middle Ages, the English Evangelicals who abolished the Slave Trade, all left their mark on Earth, precisely because their minds were occupied with Heaven.

It is since Christians have largely ceased to think of the other world that they have become so ineffective in this. Aim at Heaven and you will get earth "thrown in": aim at earth and you will get neither.

So did Father Seraphim Rose:

Christ is the only exit from this world; all other exits — sexual rapture, political utopia, economic independence — are but blind alleys in which rot the corpses of the many who have tried them.

Pope Benedict XVI likewise made the point in 1997, in what I call his "mustard seed prophecy":

Perhaps the time has come to say farewell to the idea of traditionally Catholic cultures. Maybe we are facing a new and different kind of epoch in the Church's history, where Christianity will again be characterized more and more by the mustard seed, where it will exist in small, seemingly insignificant groups that nonetheless live an intensive struggle against evil and bring the good into the world, that let God in.

So did Father Alexander Schmemann throughout his career, but most powerfully in *For the Life of the World*:

What am I going to do? What are the church and each Christian to do in this world? What is our mission?

To these questions there exist no answers in the form of practical "recipes." It all depends on thousands of factors — and, to be sure, all faculties of our human intelligence and wisdom, organization and planning, are to be constantly used. Yet — and this is the one "point" we wanted to make in these pages — "it all depends" primarily on our being real witnesses to the joy and peace of the Holy Spirit, to that new life of which we are made partakers in the Church.... It is only when in the darkness of *this* world we discern that Christ has already "filled all things with himself," and that these *things*, whatever they may be, are revealed and given to us full of meaning and beauty. A Christian is the one who, wherever he will, finds Christ and rejoices in him. And this joy *transforms* all these human plans and programs, decisions and actions, making all his mission the sacrament of the world's return to him who is the life of the world.

Of course, there's Rod Dreher's "Benedict Option":

If we want to survive, we have to return to the roots of our faith, both in thought and practice. We are going to have to learn habits of the heart forgotten by believers in the West. We are going to have to change our lives, and our approach to life, in radical ways. In short, we are going to have to be the church, without compromise, no matter what it costs....

If we are going to be for the world as Christ meant for us to be, we are going to have to spend more time away from the world, in deep prayer and substantial spiritual training, just as Jesus retreated to the desert to pray before ministering to the people. We cannot give the world what we do not have.

There's Paul Kingsnorth's "Wild Christianity":

I feel like I am being firmly pointed, day after day, back toward the green desert that forms my Christian inheritance, toward that "ardent and active solitude." Back to the song that is sung quietly through the land by its maker, the song that is in the stream running, in the mist wreathing the crags, the growling of the rooks, the thunder over the mountains. Back to the caves, to the skelligs, to the deserts green and brown, to stretch out my arms *crossfigel* and recite the great prayer of St. Patrick's Breastplate: "The light of the sun, the radiance of the moon, the splendor of fire, the speed of lightning, the swiftness of wind, the depth of the sea ..." I feel that in another time of crisis and confusion we need to go back to our roots, both literal and spiritual. To flee from the gaze of a civilized center that denies God and launches salvo after salvo daily against the human soul. To seek out a wild Christianity, which will see us praying for hours in the sea as the otters play around us. To understand—to remember—that the Earth and the world are not the same thing.

There's Father Calvin Robinson and Matt Fradd on *Pints with Aquinas*:

> ROBINSON. I don't think it's even possible for conservatives to conserve Western civilization anymore. It's up to Christians—if it is going to be conserved. I actually think it's probably too late, and Western civilization has peaked and we're on a downward trend now. Which is fine, because us Christians, we have hope in what's to come....

> FRADD. I think I've come to the opinion that Western civilization is dead.... Which is actually kind of freeing. Because you don't have to keep holding up a structure that doesn't exist. We can think of ourselves, as Pope Francis says, as medics in the field.

And we could give many more examples, from George MacDonald, G. K. Chesterton, Eberhard Arnold, Jacques Maritain, T. S. Eliot, Dorothy Day, Seraphim Rose, Alasdair MacIntyre ... The list goes on and on. Many have urged Christians to make peace with the loss of worldly power. Many have urged us to embrace our traditional role as suffering servants.

But somehow this thesis is still extremely controversial—or, at best, deeply, even willfully, misunderstood. Many great men and women are telling us to stop hiding in the pews and start making disciples of all nations. Yet somehow they're dismissed as "retreatists," "quietists," even "defeatists." Why?

Because we're afraid.

I don't mean that as an insult. Of course we're afraid. The future looks grim. I can understand why some folks would rather avert their eyes. The trouble is, fear has warped our entire worldview.

Take this whole idea of the "Culture War": the struggle between Christians and non-Christians (liberals, progressives, secularists, globalists, the LGBT lobby, and so on) for control of the West. We defend our actions because we say it's a defensive war. We're fighting to defend our churches, our families, our very way of life.

In some ways, the Culture-War mindset springs from the noblest part of our nature. We imagine we stand with Saint Bernard, who championed the Crusades and wrote: "The knight of Christ may strike with confidence and die yet more confidently, for he serves Christ when he strikes, and serves himself when he falls."

But what about Christ, who says: "Whoever slaps you on your right cheek, turn the other to him also"? And, "If anyone wants to sue you and take away your tunic, let him have your cloak also"? And "Love your enemies, bless those who curse you, do good to those who hate you, and pray for those who spitefully use you and persecute you"?

The Master refers to the Kingdom of God as a "pearl of great price." We Christians may be poor, maligned, and abused; in fact, we usually are. And yet, because we possess this pearl, we are the *haves*; those who impoverish, malign, and abuse us—they are the *have-nots*. And by persecuting us, they add to our riches. "In this you greatly rejoice," Saint Peter writes: "you have been grieved by various trials, that the genuineness of your faith, being much more precious than gold that perishes, though it is tested by fire, may be found to praise, honor, and glory at the revelation of Jesus Christ, whom having not seen you love."

This is the way of the Gospel. Persecution is to be embraced, not resisted. Our persecutors are to be loved, even pitied, rather than feared or scorned.

Yes, there are exceptions. Of course there are. But for too long, Christians have lived according to the exceptions instead of the rule. The Gospel is clear on this point: the best defense is a good offense, and the best offense is love. The first Christians understood that. It's why the *Didache* says, "Love those who hate you, and you shall not have an enemy."[5]

The Early Church possessed something else that we've since lost, something that helps to explain its commitment to the Way of Love. Fr. John Strickland calls it a "Christian anthropology," an authentically Christian understanding of what it means to be human.

For the Christian, the most important thing to understand about anyone, friend or foe, is that *he's immortal*. Here, too, I think Lewis put it best. "There are no ordinary people," he said:

> You have never talked to a mere mortal. Nations, cultures, arts, civilizations, these are mortal, and their life is to ours as the life of a gnat. But it is immortals whom we joke with, work with, marry, snub and exploit, immortal horrors or

---

[5] The *Didache* is a catechism dating back to the first century, the oldest still in existence. For the complete text, see appendix A.

everlasting splendors. This does not mean that we are to be perpetually solemn. We must play. But our merriment must be of that kind (and it is, in fact, the merriest kind) which exists between people who have, from the outset, taken each other seriously, no flippancy, no superiority, no presumption.

"The load, or weight, or burden of my neighbor's glory should be laid on my back," he said, "a load so heavy that only humility can carry it, and the backs of the proud will be broken."

We're going to live forever, every last one of us. The only question is whether we'll live happily ever after with God, or not-so-happily ever after with the Devil. And how we spend our time on Earth determines, in no small part, how we'll spend eternity.

Those who persecute us (as Saint Peter said) only smooth our way to Paradise. But they do unspeakable harm to their own souls in the process. They trade the priceless pearl for a handful of costume jewelry. That's why the Master tells us to love them, to pray for them, to pity them. It's why He cried out from the cross, "Father, forgive them, for they do not know what they do"

To imitate Christ, as the first Christians knew, means to plead on behalf of our enemies. Because we have only one true Enemy: the Devil. As for the rest, those who *seem* to be our enemies — progressives, secularists, whatever — they're our brothers and, as Saint Paul says, the "slaves of sin."

We, too, were once slaves of sin. Through no merit of our own, Christ broke our chains and called us His friends. How can we spurn those who remain enslaved, merely because they've yet to gain their freedom? If we do, we're no better than the wicked servant who begged the Master to forgive his debt of ten thousand talents but wouldn't forgive the fellow who owed him a hundred denarii.

And Jesus, in His unfathomable goodness, not only breaks our chains: He invites us to assist in His great work of salvation. This is what we call the "Great Commission":

> All authority has been given to me in heaven and on earth. Go therefore and make disciples of all the nations, baptizing them in the name of the Father and of the Son and of the Holy Spirit, teaching them to observe all things that I have commanded you; and lo, I am with you always, even to the end of the age.

In this sense, the "Culture War" is the *antithesis* of the Great Commission. One calls us to fight to the death; the other, to lay down our lives. One tells us to fear our enemies; the other tells us to love them so they become our friends. One is based on the wisdom of man; the other, on the foolishness of God.

Deep down in my bones, I believe this is why He's letting us lose. We Christians keep saying, "War, war," when there is no war, only defeat. For the last five hundred years (at least!), we've been inventing new and ingenious ways to save Christendom from collapsing in on itself. Every single one of them has failed. Maybe it's time to try things God's way.

Unfortunately, I don't think we'll be able to make that choice of our own volition. Only persecution can shatter the chains of fear and pride that keep us bound to ideology. Only suffering will break the hardness of our hearts and allow us to see the world through God's eyes: the eyes of love. I'm afraid that only when we're locked away in our own gulag—whatever form it takes—will we be granted a revelation like Solzhenitsyn's:

> Gradually, it was disclosed to me that the line separating good and evil passes not through states, nor between

classes, nor between political parties—but right through every human heart—and then through all human hearts.... And even within hearts overwhelmed by evil, one small bridgehead of good is retained. And even in the best of all hearts, there remains ... an unuprooted small corner of evil.

Suffering has a way of freeing us from the manacles of our own egos. It brings our own failures into sharp relief; it also has a way of obscuring the faults of others. It makes us want to love—and to be loved.

We have forgotten how to love, and so we've forgotten God; we've forgotten God, and so we've forgotten how to love. In order to bring our neighbors to Christ, we have to love them; and the best way to love them is to bring them to Christ. These are not two tasks, and this is not a zero-sum game. The Faith is a gift from the Father, which He asks us to share—and, the more we share it, the more He gives it to us.

But, again, I'm afraid that it's only by suffering that the Church will learn how to love again. And only by re-crucifying the Body of Christ will the powers of this world fall down like the centurion and cry, "Truly this was the Son of God."

So our task is not to fight for control of the West. Our task is to seed the West by our blood, just like Christ and the Apostles and the Virgins and the Martyrs. If it's God's will that Christendom be born again, then it must be born again, in suffering.

Ours is only to answer hate with love—since, as Saint Charbel said, "The only weapon is love."

5

The Universal Call to Mysticism

The inmost thoughts of man shall give praise to thee,
the remainder of man's mind shall keep feast to thee.

—Psalm 75:10

The devout Christian of the future will either be
a mystic, or he will cease to be anything at all.

—Karl Rahner

If you read the Greek Fathers, you'll notice that another word pops up over and over. The word is *phronema*, and it means "mentality" or "mindset." The Eastern churches place a strong emphasis on developing a Christian phronema. It's not enough, they say, simply to memorize Christ's teaching. You have to learn how to think the way Christ thinks, to see as He sees, to feel as He feels. You have to put on the "mind of Christ," as Saint Paul calls it (1 Cor. 2:16). Every part of our selves must be converted, baptized, and redeemed, our minds and our bodies, our hearts and our souls.

As with all secular ideologies, the conservative phronema feels a tension between Christ's command to love our neighbor and Augustine's command to change the times. Hence the idea of the "Culture War."

The first Christians felt no such tension. On the contrary. In the very first verse of the *Didache*, the Fathers say,

> The way of life, then, is this: First, you shall love God who made you; second, love your neighbor as yourself, and do not do to another what you would not want done to you. And of these sayings the teaching is this: Bless those who curse you, and pray for your enemies, and fast for those who persecute you. For what reward is there for loving those who

love you? Do not the Gentiles do the same? But love those who hate you, and you shall not have an enemy.

"Love those who hate you, and you shall not have an enemy." We've quoted this line already, but it's worth repeating over and over. Because this is how a Christian thinks. This is the phronema of the Fathers of the Church. This is the mindset that won the West. It is the mindset that can win it back. It is the only mindset that can win it back.

But what does it look like in practice? What should we actually *do*? I would break our "praxis" into four parts, per the book of Tobit: (1) prayer, (2) fasting, (3) almsgiving, and (4) righteousness.

I. Prayer

For centuries, Westerners' faith was sustained largely by institutions, by communities, both temporal and spiritual. Today, however, many feel alienated from those institutions, and the communities they engendered are falling apart. Whether it's a Roman Catholic talking about the "visible Church" or a Congregationalist talking about his local parish, they're usually singing the same tune. We all feel more spiritually isolated than our parents and grandparents did. In fact, ours is probably the most isolated generation of Western Christians since the fourth century—and never in the last seventeen hundred years have we needed their help so badly.

We won't survive the present crisis without true friends to journey with us, and true shepherds to lead us on our way. (More on that in chapter 10.) Yet even those companions won't be enough. What each of us needs more than anything else is a deep, intimate, personal relationship with Jesus Christ.

I know. Anyone who uses the phrase "personal relationship with Jesus" is just asking for eyerolls. But it's true. In fact, it's essential. It's everything.

Remember Saint Ignatius of Antioch's letter to the Church in Rome, which he wrote just days before he was killed by the pagans. "Pardon me, brethren," he pleads. "Do not hinder me from living, do not wish to keep me in a state of death; and while I desire to belong to God, do not give me over to the world." "And let no one ... envy me that I should attain to Jesus Christ," he says. "Let fire and the cross; let the crowds of wild beasts; let tearings, breakings, and dislocations of bones; let cutting off of members; let shatterings of the whole body; and let all the dreadful torments of the devil come upon me. Only let me attain to Jesus Christ."

Both in life and in death, Ignatius had only one desire: to see God face-to-face. This was the end of all his worldly striving, of his prayers, of his preaching, and of his death as a martyr.

Really, this is something we find everywhere in the writings of all the Church Fathers. For every last one of them, to be a Christian meant having faith, not in certain rites or teachings, but in a *Person*: the Lord Jesus. A Christian is someone who seeks to know Christ, to love Christ, to imitate Christ, and, if given the chance, to die for Christ.

"For now we see through a glass, darkly," writes Saint Paul, "but then face to face." Yet how many of us see Him even darkly in this life? How many of us search for His face in that glass? How many of us really believe we could, even if we tried?

Unfortunately, sheer elitism prevents many of us from seeking Him out. When we hear someone talk about having a "personal relationship" with the Master, we assume he goes to a trendy megachurch where all the pastors wear beards and black T-shirts. In fact, even many Catholics seem to take pride in their impersonal relationship with God. As Julia Yost wrote in the *New York Times* not long ago, " 'Authentic' internal conversion is not a Catholic demand but a Protestant one."

That's not true, not even in the best of times. And these are not the best of times.

We might say that Christendom was like a dam. It diverted the current of the secular world toward the Church. Even those with little or no supernatural faith were swept along toward the Gate of Life. But now the dam has been washed away, and the current carries us to the Gate of Death. To reach the Gate of Life now requires constant and careful struggle, a renewed effort, day by day, hour by hour. Every moment of our lives requires an "authentic conversion" and a conscious decision to conform ourselves to Christ. If we lag, even for a minute, we'll be carried further back downstream.

Without God, such constancy would be impossible. With Him, anything is possible.

But how do we tap into those graces? Prayer.

In the Christian tradition, we usually divide prayer into two categories: liturgical and personal. *Liturgical prayer* refers to any form of set prayer that we practice collectively. Usually this prayer takes place in church—for instance, the Holy Mass. But it may also take place at home. When Catholics practice the Liturgy of the Hours or Orthodox Christians chant the kathismas, their prayers are mystically joined with the prayers of the whole Church, everywhere, all over the world, throughout all time and space.

Liturgical prayer is essential for maintaining any true *ekklesia*. I don't want to minimize its importance, especially not in this day and age. But, more and more, faithful Christians are remembering the need for personal prayer.

Personal prayer is a catch-all term for any prayer that we perform … well, personally. It aims specifically to deepen our relationship with Christ. Anyone can achieve such a relationship with Him because God wants all of us to have such a relationship—every last one of us. He made the first move, so to speak, by creating us in His own image.

Mark my words: if we fail to cultivate this relationship with Christ, we will not weather the coming storm. Saint Ignatius of Antioch made that much abundantly clear. We won't fight for Christ unless we know Him. We won't die for Christ unless we love Him.

There are countless ways to engage in personal prayer. Here, though, I'd like to discuss three examples and their importance to modern Christians.

First is the Jesus Prayer. The Jesus Prayer was formulated by the Desert Fathers in response to Saint Paul's command to "pray always." It has two essential parts: an invocation of the Holy Name and a plea for forgiveness. It has many forms. The traditional form is "Lord Jesus Christ, have mercy"; but in the English-speaking world the most common form is "Jesus Christ, Son of God, have mercy on me, a sinner." Yet the Jesus Prayer may be as short as two words ("Jesus, mercy"). The idea is that, by practicing the Jesus Prayer often enough, usually in sync with one's breathing, it becomes a "prayer of the heart": a prayer that rises from our hearts frequently, effortlessly, spontaneously, almost automatically.

As modern masters of the Jesus Prayer are careful to point out, it isn't like a Buddhist mantra. It's not a phrase we repeat in order to induce some kind of trance, or to clear our minds, or to bring about inner peace. It *does* often bring about inner peace, of course. But that's only a "side benefit." The end of all true prayer is union with God.

Metropolitan Kallistos Ware (of blessed memory) put it nicely:

We are taught, when reciting the Jesus Prayer, to avoid so far as possible any specific image or picture. In the words of Saint Gregory of Nyssa, "The Bridegroom is present, but he is not seen." ... But, while turning aside from images, we are to concentrate our full attention upon, or rather within, the words. The Jesus Prayer is not just a hypnotic incantation but a meaningful phrase, an invocation addressed to another Person. Its object is not relaxation but alertness, not waking slumber but living prayer. And so the Jesus Prayer is not to be said mechanically but with inward purpose; yet at the same time the words should be pronounced without tension, violence, or undue emphasis. The string round our spiritual parcel should be taut, not left hanging slack; yet it should not be drawn so tight as to cut the edges of the package.

The point of the Jesus Prayer is to make us aware of the omnipresence of Christ, and to speak with Him, heart to Heart. Of course, there are many ways of speaking to Christ. We can simply have a conversation with Him about our failures, our fears, our hopes, our hatreds, and our loves. And this, too, is a necessary part of the spiritual life. This is personal prayer in its raw form. But, with the Jesus Prayer, there's an implicit recognition that we don't *need* to tell the Lord our failures, hopes, and so forth. He already knows our hearts, even better than we do ourselves. We couldn't keep a secret from Him if we tried (and we do try).

The Jesus Prayer is prayer distilled to its essential elements. It invites us to empty ourselves of all words, images, and feelings and of our worries, our ambitions, even our powers of imagination, to make our whole selves receptive to the Holy Spirit. And we do that by concentrating our selves—mind, body, heart, and soul—entirely on the immanent presence of Christ. Then we utter this short prayer, which is really two prayers, the two most necessary: a profession of faith ("Lord Jesus Christ, Son of God") and an act of contrition ("have mercy on me, a sinner").

The Jesus Prayer can be prayed by anyone and should be prayed by everyone—and that's the point. Our sins and weaknesses are what divide us, not only from one another but from God. Buried within ourselves, however, in the fathomless abyss—in the deep that calls unto deep—we see the divine spark. This is where He comes to dwell within us. This is where we find His image, His likeness. And it's here, in the kingdom of the heart, that we're closest not only to God but to one another.

St. Seraphim of Sarov, that great master of the Jesus Prayer, made this point beautifully. One day, someone asked how he could peer so deeply into the human heart. "No, no, my joy," he said (St. Seraphim called everyone his joy). "The human heart is open to God alone and when one approaches it one finds oneself on the brink of an abyss."

In this way, the Jesus Prayer teaches us to love not only God but also our neighbor. The more clearly we see God's likeness in ourselves, the more clearly we're able to see His likeness in our neighbors. And the more we recognize that likeness in our neighbors, the more we love them. The more we love our neighbors, the more we desire to serve them. We can love our enemies and pray for those who persecute us *only if we can gaze into their abysses*, as Christ did. Then we can say, as He did, "Father, forgive them, for they do not know what they do."

The Jesus Prayer is an *apophatic prayer*: a kind of prayer that we begin by clearing our minds of all thoughts, feelings, and images. This is in contrast to *kataphatic prayer*, which reaches out to God using our rational minds, our emotions, even our imaginations. The best example of kataphatic prayer, I think, is *Lectio Divina*, or "divine reading."

Like the Jesus Prayer, we owe the practice of Lectio Divina to the monastic fathers. Monks would devote a portion of their day (usually an hour, sometimes more) to meditating on Holy Scripture. But they wouldn't simply read through a certain book of the Bible. Rather, they would choose a small section (usually a chapter, sometimes more) and read it over and over.

If they chose Luke 1:26-38, for instance, they might imagine the scene playing out. What was Mary doing before Gabriel arrived? Did he come in a flash of light, or did he simply appear before her? Why does the evangelist say that she was "greatly troubled"? Was she simply startled? Was she afraid? Had she ever felt some inkling that, before God began His great work of creation, He had chosen her to be His Mother, that He had kept her immaculate, spotless, free from all sin, from the moment of her conception?

The aim of Lectio Divina is threefold. The first aim, of course, is to become familiar with Scripture. Usually the monks would try to memorize a certain portion of what they read, if only a single verse.

The second aim is to "baptize" the imagination. Lectio Divina helps us to keep our thoughts trained on heavenly things. If you watch a lot of *South Park*, you're going to think a lot about *South Park*. You're going to quote *South Park* a lot, if only to yourself. Your sense of humor will become more like *South Park*'s. You'll start to absorb the values, the worldview, of *South Park*. Lectio Divina does the same thing, except with Holy Scripture instead of *South Park*.

The third aim is the aim of all personal prayer: by practicing Lectio Divina, we unite ourselves more closely to God. We experience Him personally, individually, through His sacred Word. When we immerse ourselves in Scripture, we immerse ourselves in God. And, again, it's only through a personal encounter with God that our faith will endure the post-Christian West.

If you want to know more about the specific practice of the Jesus Prayer and Lectio Divina, there are plenty of terrific resources.[6]

---

[6] I recommend Fathers Acklin and Hicks's *Personal Prayer: A Guide for Receiving the Father's Love.*

But there's still one other form of prayer we have to discuss. It was essential to the building of Christendom, and it will be essential to the rebuilding Christendom. Father Gabriel of Saint Mary Magdalen called it *apostolic prayer*:

> When Jesus died on the Cross for us, the redemption of mankind became an accomplished fact.... What still remains to be done is the application of these graces to each individual soul; and, it is for this that God wishes our collaboration. He wants it so much that He has made the granting of certain graces, necessary for our salvation and that of others, dependent upon our prayers. In other words, by the merits of Jesus, grace, God's infinite mercy, is ready to be poured out abundantly into men's souls, but it will not be poured out unless there is someone who raises supplicating hands to heaven, asking for it. If prayer does not ascend to the throne of the Most High, grace will not be granted. This explains the absolute necessity for apostolic prayer and its great efficacy.

"There is no substitute for prayer," Father Gabriel warns, "because prayer draws grace directly from its source, God. Our activity, our words, and works can prepare the ground for grace, but if we do not pray, it will not come down to refresh souls."

Think about what this means. God the Son died to redeem the whole world; and as the Master says, "If you have faith as a mustard seed, you will say to this mountain, 'Move from here to there,' and it will move; and nothing will be impossible for you." Every single human being on the planet could be converted tomorrow, if only we asked for it. There's grace enough, and then some.

We might assent to this in our heads. But do we know it in our hearts?

How much time do we spend in apostolic prayer? How much time compared with watching the news or arguing about politics? Answer honestly, and then ask yourself: Do you put your trust more in God or in princes—or in yourself?

Believe me, I'm as guilty as anyone. I trust God about as far as I can throw Him. I say "Christ is Lord" with my lips—but in my heart I believe it's up to me to save the world. This is called the heresy of *activism*. It's the opposite of *quietism*, the belief that God wants Christians to be completely passive. You hear the word *quietist* thrown around quite a lot in conservative circles, especially when the Benedict Option is mentioned. But I'd guess that, for every true quietist in America, there are five hundred thousand "activists"—and yet you never hear activism described as a sin.

Besides, as Father Gabriel points out, apostolic prayer is the opposite of quietism. All good work, good statecraft included, is achieved by grace, and apostolic prayer draws grace directly from its source. Would you rather drink from a well or from living water?

II. Fasting

St. Paul lays out the purpose for fasting very nicely in his letter to the Romans. "For I know that in me ... nothing good dwells," he laments. "The good that I will to do, I do not do; but the evil I will not to do, that I practice."

When we rely on our own selves, our wisdom, our strength, our discipline, our charm, we're useless. In fact, we're worse than useless. We become instruments of evil. By committing the sin of pride, we ally ourselves to the Enemy. We return to the slavery of sin.

According to Paul, we have only two choices: either we're slaves to sin or we're "slaves of righteousness for holiness."

How do we become enslaved to righteousness to God? Through fasting. By fasting, we say with John the Baptist: "He must increase, but I must decrease." We starve not only our bodies but our appetites. We learn to be ruled by a desire not for food or sex or wealth or power but for holiness.

Really, it's no use putting on the "mind of Christ" if we're at the mercy of our bellies. By fasting, we train our bodies to conform to our Christian phronema. We begin to think as Christ would think, to act as Christ would act. We empty ourselves so that we can say with Paul, "I am crucified with Christ: nevertheless I live; yet not I, but Christ liveth in me." In the Christian East, this self-emptying is known as *kenosis*.

What's tragic is that most Westerners, including most Christians, think that fasting is supposed to make us miserable. It's not just that they think fasting *does* make us miserable: they think that misery is the whole point of it. But this kind of thinking comes from a worldly phronema. It's a lie straight from the Father of Lies. It's one of his finest works.

We know that the most joyful saints, from Francis of Assisi to Seraphim of Sarov, were the most zealous penitents. It wasn't that they hated their bodies; they weren't gnostics. Rather, they loved what their bodies could be if they broke the shackles of sin. They drove out their carnal appetites to make room for God. "Do not be gloomy while you are being healed," writes Saint Basil in his first homily on fasting. Rather, "be cheerful since the physician has given you sin-destroying medicine."

As Cardinal Newman points out, we can't develop a Christian phronema unless we also practice fasting and penance:

Till we, in a certain sense, detach ourselves from our bodies, our minds will not be in a state to receive divine impressions, and to exert heavenly aspirations. A smooth and easy life, an uninterrupted enjoyment of the goods of

Providence, full meals, soft raiment, well-furnished homes, the pleasures of sense, the feeling of security, the consciousness of wealth, these, and the like, if we are not careful, choke up all the avenues of the soul, through which the light and breath of heaven might come to us.

A hard life is, alas! no certain method of becoming spiritually minded, but it is one out of the means by which Almighty God makes us so. We must, at least at seasons, defraud ourselves of nature, if we would not be defrauded of grace.

If we attempt to force our minds into a loving and devotional temper, without this preparation, it is too plain what will follow, the grossness and coarseness, the affectation, the effeminacy, the unreality, the presumption, the hollowness (suffer me, my brethren, while I say plainly, but seriously, what I mean) in a word, what Scripture calls the Hypocrisy, which we see around us; that state of mind in which the reason, seeing what we should be, and the conscience enjoining it, and the heart being unequal to it, some or other pretense is set up, by way of compromise, that men may say, "Peace, peace, when there is no peace."

We might even go so far as to say that we Christians have devolved into mere "conservatives" in no small part because we've failed to fast. We cling so bitterly to worldly influence because we're so terrified of persecution, deprivation, and ostracization. We're afraid of pain and embarrassment. We shrink from even the mildest inconvenience. And this fear clouds our judgment. It warps our entire worldview.

Here we come to the paradox of freedom. Only by becoming Christ's slaves can we put on the mind of Christ. But, once we develop a Christian phronema, Christ sets us free. Holiness itself is freedom. "No longer do I call you servants," the Master says, "for a servant does not know what his master is doing; but I have called you friends, for all things that I heard from My Father I have made known to you." Freedom really is a state of mind, the Christian state of mind.

Fasting is also critical for attaining what Nicholas Nassim Taleb calls *antifragility*. "Antifragility is beyond resilience or robustness," he says. Antifragile things (and people) "benefit from shocks; they thrive and grow when exposed to volatility, randomness, disorder, and stressors and love adventure, risk, and uncertainty."

The martyrs and missionaries of old were antifragile. They not only accepted life's sufferings: they embraced them. They took real joy in the privilege of being able to suffer and fight and die for the sake of Christ's Church. Life's trials weren't something to complain about. They were God's way of allowing us to share in His glory, His way of making us vehicles for His strength.

Think of Saint Lawrence, who, while being roasted alive by the Romans, called out: "Turn me over. I'm done on this side." Think of Saint Thomas More, who, walking to the scaffold, said to his executioner: "See me safe up. Coming down, I can shift for myself." Think of Saint Ignatius of Antioch begging his flock not to deprive him of the "tearings" and "shatterings" of martyrdom, by which he would attain Jesus Christ.

These men were spiritually rugged. They were antifragile. Even as they were *literally* in the process of being executed, they never lost sight of their joy, which is one of the gifts of the Holy Ghost.

Joy, I think, is the mark of an antifragile Christian. Yet so many Christians today are both fragile and joyless.

Most of us can't be bothered to fulfill the basic obligations of our Faith, such as going to church every Sunday. Just thirty-two percent of Christians, according to the Pew Research Center, say that sex between unmarried couples is unacceptable. In other words, over three-quarters no longer think fornication is a sin. Even when Pew surveyed only regular churchgoers, just forty-three percent (less than half!) say that sex outside of marriage is always wrong.

Did this shift in thinking come about as the result of deep theological probing? I doubt it. We're just getting soft. And just to be clear: I'm not throwing shade at the many Christians who struggle, painfully, with sins of the flesh. I'm talking about the ones who don't struggle at all, the ones who've given up.

I spent ten years working as a journalist, covering the affairs of Church and State from a Christian perspective. Over the course of that decade, I noticed the tone of Christian media growing increasingly shrill. There was a lot more whining, a lot more complaining, a lot more grandstanding. Pundits were more likely to spread gossip and fling *ad hominems*, not only at other journalists and politicians but also at the clergy; and the clergy themselves happily fling them back. The Catholic Church is overrun with celebrity priests and bishops (both "conservative" and "liberal") who gather hordes of devoted followers by loudly dissenting from Church teaching or insulting their superiors. And we, the hordes, find this shrillness creeping into our own conversations.

All of this shows how very coddled we are. We're personally offended by the existence of folks whose opinions differ from ours. We feel entitled to say whatever's on our mind. If someone disagrees with us, or suggests that we use more diplomatic language, or points out that we might keep some of our opinions to ourselves, we go around telling folks we've been "canceled." We're all snowflakes now.

But this catty, flippant behavior betrays another weakness because grandstanding of this kind is obviously counterproductive.

It alienates those who might otherwise agree with us while also making it clear to our opponents that we're acting in bad faith. Worst of all, the point isn't to change hearts and minds, or even to browbeat or intimidate. These folks don't really expect to *win*. They're not even trying.

This, in turn, shows a lack of seriousness about the crisis we face—and highlights another kind of fragility. We're not capable of talking about this crisis with patience, kindness, humility, and self-control (four more gifts of the Holy Ghost).

But fasting breaks our slavery to our appetites. It makes us strong in the Faith. It gives us clarity of vision. It teaches us to master our emotions. When the *real* persecution begins, we will need to be strong.

III. Almsgiving

In the Christian tradition, giving alms to the poor is one of the seven Corporal Works of Mercy. The other six are to feed the hungry, to give drink to the thirsty, to shelter the homeless, to tend the sick, to visit the imprisoned, and to bury the dead. The list varies slightly from one source to the next. But the idea is that we Christians are called to serve our neighbors' bodies as well as their souls. We have a duty to relieve their suffering, physical as well as spiritual.

I like to illustrate this point by talking about something I call the *soup-kitchen fallacy*. Every once in a while, you'll hear some well-meaning priest or pastor give a homily on charity, or Christian love. Almost inevitably, he'll say something like: "Of course, charity means more than giving change to beggars or volunteering in soup kitchens."

Now, he's not wrong. There's more to charity than good deeds. But there isn't *less* to charity than good deeds, if you see what I mean.

Put it this way. If you're a Christian, and you believe the Lord's command to love your neighbor, and your neighbor is hungry—what could be more natural than to give him a bowl of soup?

This is what Christ meant by the parable of the sheep and the goats. The sheep are the righteous who, at the Last Judgment, will hear the Shepherd say, "Come, you blessed of my Father, inherit the kingdom prepared for you from the foundation of the world. For I was hungry and you gave me food; I was thirsty and you gave me drink; I was a stranger and you took me in; I *was* naked and you clothed me; I was sick and you visited me; I was in prison and you came to me."

The sheep will say, "Lord, when did we do these things for you?" And He'll answer, "Inasmuch as you did it to one of the least of these my brethren, you did it to me."

The goats, meanwhile, are the unrighteous. These are the ones who *didn't* feed Him when He was hungry, who *didn't* give Him water when He was thirsty ... At the Last Judgment, He'll say, "Depart from me, you cursed, into the everlasting fire prepared for the devil and his angels." The goats will bleat, "Lord, when did we fail to do these things for you?" And He'll answer, "Inasmuch as you did not do it to one of the least of these, you did not do it to me."

Clearly, good deeds aren't an "optional extra" in the Christian life. They're fundamental. The heart of Christianity is a loving God, a God who is Himself love. For us, love is the first principle. It's the reason for everything. We exist *in* love, *by* love, *through* love, *for* love. And the most ordinary manifestation of love is the desire to relieve another's suffering, even if it means taking that person's suffering upon ourselves, as Christ did.

But the Works of Mercy are also indispensable to the Great Commission. The witness of charity, no less than the witness of martyrdom, made a deep impression on the Romans. It gave credence to the Christian faith. "Thus, in the late second century," recalls David Bentley Hart,

> Tertullian could justly boast that whereas the money donated to the temples of the old gods was squandered on feasts and drink, with their momentary pleasures, the money given to churches was used to care for the impoverished and the abandoned, to grant even the poorest decent burials, and to provide for the needs for the elderly.

Tertullian also famously said: "It is mainly the deeds of a love so noble that lead many to put a brand upon us. 'See,' they say, 'how they love one another.'"[7]

Some readers might protest that Christians give more to charity than any other demographic in America, that the Catholic Church is the largest charitable organization in the world, and so on. That's all true. But like everything else in the modern world, our charity is, to a large extent, *professionalized*. We outsource our good deeds to nonprofits, which employ armies of social workers. We support these nonprofits through our donations (though, according to the Barna Group, fewer than three percent of churchgoers give ten percent of their income to the Church and other worthy causes, as God commands us to do, insofar as we are able).

By outsourcing the Works of Mercy to professionals, we put our souls in jeopardy. We also obfuscate our charitable witness. This witness was crucial in winning the West for Christ. It will be no less crucial in winning it back. Christendom won't recover until the pagans take up their old refrain: "See how they love one another."

---

[7] Tertullian, *Apology* 39.

IV. Righteousness

As I was writing this book, my friend Father Robert McTeigue made a very important observation (as he's wont to do). Father pointed out that, when folks talk about a "Second Pentecost" or a "New Apostolic Age," they're usually doing one of two things: either they are trying to introduce some error or novelty into the Church, or they are trying to deflect attention from the dismal state of the Church. They pretend that the decline of Christianity is actually a *good thing*. They say that God is calling us back to a humbler faith, a simpler way of life. Never mind the heresies that are tearing the Church apart, from both within and without; pay no attention to that apostate behind the curtain.

For many of us, the most disturbing manifestation of our crisis is the push by liberal clerics and theologians to "baptize" certain sins. All of the mainline Protestant denominations now enthusiastically approve of fornication, divorce, and homosexuality. Most are tolerant of abortion; some are passionately pro-choice.

Many traditional Protestants have opted to form breakaway churches, such as the Anglican Church in North America. Many others, who aren't so wedded to these older expressions of Protestantism, are embracing "nondenominationalism" instead. An optimist would point out that old-school Protestants now outnumber modernist Protestants—and that should certainly give us heart! Yet conservative Protestants form a dwindling percentage of the overall population. Card-carrying Modernists may be rare, but few Americans still believe in "Christian values," and that includes most Christians. No: despite their many virtues, these conservative Protestants haven't been able to stem the tide of secularism and apostasy.

Of course, the Orthodox are not faring much better. Nor are the Catholics. There is now a small yet powerful clique of bishops, both in the United States and in Europe, who publicly dissent from both historical Christianity and the Vatican on issues such as human sexuality. Meanwhile, the Catholic laity is even *less* likely to obey our Church's moral precepts than our separated brethren. According to one survey, 98 percent of Catholics simply ignore the Church's prohibition on artificial contraception.

I'm sure none of this is news to you. The question is: *What can we do about it?*

To be clear, I don't mean, "What should the clergy do about it?" (I don't think they'll read this book.) I don't mean, "What should the next Constantine do about it?" I mean, "What can we, the lay faithful, do, right here, right now?"

Here's what: love. Just as we can reclaim the West only through love, so too we can reclaim the Church only through love.

Think of Saint Francis of Assisi. By the time Francis was born in 1181, Europe had already begun its decline into decadence. (That decline would culminate about 150 years later in the Renaissance.) One day, Francis was praying in a falling-down old chapel called San Damiano. Suddenly, an icon of Jesus on the cross began to speak to him. "Rebuild my Church," the Lord said to him. Francis, in his simplicity, immediately went around begging for bricks and mortar. It soon became clear that Our Lord had bigger plans for Francis.

As he discerned his new vocation, Francis was inspired by two passages from Scripture. The first was from Luke's Gospel: "Take nothing for the journey, neither staff nor bag nor bread nor money; and do not have two tunics apiece." The second was from Mark: "Go into all the world and preach the gospel to every creature."

That's exactly what Francis did. He stripped naked and walked into the woods, sharing the Good News with anyone who would listen. His first audience was a band of robbers. They beat him until he lost consciousness and then dumped his bleeding body in a ditch.

The sorry state of the Catholic Church had already inspired a reaction from the Waldensians, a pro-Protestant sect that rejected clerical authority and stressed the need for apostolic poverty. In the early days of his ministry, Francis was often mistaken for a Waldensian. Whenever he arrived in a new village, mobs of loyal Catholics would drive him out with stones and sticks. Francis was no Waldensian, though. In the few writings he left behind, he repeatedly stressed the need for loyalty to the Church, to her priests, and to her teachings.

But Francis didn't preach against Waldensianism either. He wasn't a theologian. Rather, he and his bands of followers—which grew by the day—traveled around Italy giving food to the poor, healing lepers, and urging the faithful to repent of their sins.

We remember Francis best for his love of nature. We've all seen pictures of him preaching to a flock of birds, the birds sitting in rapt attention. The hagiographers also tell us about Francis's visit to the village of Gubbio. A giant wolf lived in the woods just outside the town, and every day the beast stole sheep and cows from the local farmers and killed anyone who tried to stop it.

They say that Francis sought out the wolf's cave. When the beast rushed him, he made the Sign of the Cross, and the wolf came to heel. Francis then admonished the wolf for treating its neighbors so cruelly. He insisted that it must beg for its food, as Francis and his followers did. For then on, the beast went meekly from shop to shop, eating scraps from the butchers' table. Today, the Wolf of Gubbio is honored as one of the first Franciscan friars.

The biographies of Saint Francis are filled with such stories. My favorite is a bit less dramatic. Bonaventure recalls how, one day, Francis was traipsing through the wild, singing his troubadour songs, when he came to a clearing where a babbling brook passed through a meadow in full flower. Francis plopped himself down on the ground, took out his lunch—a piece of stale bread—and began to eat. "What a treasure we have here," he cried. "What a treasure!"

Today, Francis is the most popular saint in the world, second only to the Virgin Mary. Even the most virulent anti-Christian finds it hard not to love the Little Poor Man. As early as the 1930s, Ronald Knox was poking fun at progressives who admire Saint Francis yet openly scorn the Church ("What meekness, what cheerfulness, what love of animals!... Not a bit like a Roman Catholic").

Yet, if anything, Francis was an even bigger celebrity in his own lifetime. His ordinary, Guido, was the archetype of a corrupt Catholic bishop. He lived in a sprawling palace on the hills above Assisi and came to town only to extract rent from his serfs. Yet, after meeting Francis, Guido threw in his lot with the Franciscans. Not long after, Francis won over Pope Innocent III, thanks to his friend Cardinal Ugolino di Conti, the future Pope Greory IX. Both pontiffs protected the nascent Franciscan Order from its enemies both within and outside the Church.

Then, in the middle of the Fifth Crusade, Francis traveled to the Middle East. He hoped to convert the Egyptian sultan, Al-Kamil, to Christianity. He believed that, by winning over the Muslims' commander, he could free the Holy Land and save millions of souls in one fell swoop. Francis spent several weeks as a guest in the sultan's court, preaching to Al-Kamil and debating his imams. His mission failed (alas), but Islamic sources from this time are rife with stories of the Christian monk who wandered into their camp one day and demanded to see the guy in charge.

What is perhaps most extraordinary, however, was Francis's popularity among the Waldensians. If you've never heard of Peter Waldo or his followers, blame the Little Poor Man. In fact, if you've ever wondered why the Reformation never spread into southern Europe, here's your answer: the Franciscans proved by their actions, by their very way of life, that it was possible to be a true Christian *and* a faithful Catholic.

That's not to trivialize the theological differences between Catholics and Protestants. But a recurring theme in Church history is that heresy and apostasy are thwarted not by polemicists or apologists or inquisitors but by *holiness*.

Here's another example. During the tenth century, a heresy known as Bogomilism arose in the Eastern Church. In many ways, the Bogomils and the Waldensians were cut from the same cloth. The Bogomils' movement was a reaction against the cold, formal spiritualty that flourished throughout the Eastern Roman Empire. For centuries, the Byzantines campaigned against the Bogomils, but with little success. Then along came a monk named Gregory Palamas.

Gregory was the scion of an elite family who had spent time on Mount Athos, two prerequisites for high office in the Eastern Church. But according to whispers at court, Gregory was a secret Bogomil.

It was true that Gregory had a great deal of sympathy for the Bogomils. He agreed that, by itself, Byzantine liturgical prayer could be too rigid and impersonal. And like them, he longed for an intimate relationship with the living God. But Gregory's solution was to become a champion of *hesychasm*: the mystical tradition of the Eastern Church that centers on the Jesus Prayer.

In addition, Gregory would often go into the mountains where the Bogomils had their strongholds and spend days arguing with their priests. Gregory praised them for their devotion to the Gospel (the Bogomils refused to use any formal prayer except the Our Father). But he also insisted that no true Christian could reject the Church, her bishops, her priests, and her magisterial faith. Before too long, whole villages would convert to orthodoxy. Gregory would then accompany the Bogomil leaders back to the imperial city, where they would make a formal act of submission to the Patriarch of Constantinople.

Western Christians tend to be skeptical of Gregory Palamas's strategy of evangelization; and Eastern Christians aren't usually too keen on Francis of Assisi's approach. And yet the two have quite a bit in common. They both lived during a time of revolt against traditional Christianity. Both recognized that such revolts stemmed, in no small part, from the corruption of Church authorities. And both defended the traditional Faith by beating the heretics at their own game: Francis fasted more than the Waldensians; Gregory prayed more than the Bogomils. Francis and Gregory responded to the crisis in the Church by offering a deeper witness to the Gospel.

In that sense, we might say that Francis and Gregory were *fundamentalists*. They weren't exactly conservatives. They didn't rigidly uphold the status quo. But they weren't liberals either. They adamantly refused to break with Church teaching or with Church authorities. Instead, they sought to call both factions, both conservatives and liberals, back to the fundamentals of Christianity.

To put it another way, Francis and Gregory refused to engage the crisis on its own terms. They didn't pick a side: they picked both sides — and neither. They didn't try to find some mushy "center ground"; nor did they try to carve out some "third way." They just went back to the basics.

What we need now, I think, aren't polemicists or apologists. We need fundamentalists like Francis and Gregory. We need men and women who will heal the wounds in the Church by offering a *lived witness* to the fundamentals of Christianity. These men and women will pray and delight in it; they will fast and spread joy; they will serve the poor, the sick, and the imprisoned; they will live in righteousness; they will love their enemies; they will pray for those who persecute them; and, all the while, they will share the Good News of the risen Lord.

These men and women will heal the Church by re-evangelizing her with their lives—and only then will the Church be well enough to re-evangelize the West.

6

I, Evangelist

My mouth shall proclaim thy righteousness,
thy salvation all the day long, for I know nothing
about the worldly business of men."

—Psalm 70:15

For Christ plays in ten thousand faces.

—Gerard Manley Hopkins

Historically, the E-word meant sharing the Gospel with non-Christians. Today, Evangelization means everything but. Sure, Protestants talk a lot about "evangelicalism"; Catholics write much about the "New Evangelization." Yet, whatever the merits of those movements, neither bears more than a passing resemblance to real, hundred-proof evangelism.

The trouble is, both evangelicalism and the New Evangelization are products of mass media. True evangelism, by contrast, is personal, intimate, raw, and self-giving. It's embarrassing to stand on a street corner asking strangers if they want to learn about Jesus. That's why "real Christians" scoff at it. Yet it's also why fringe sects—such as the Mormons and Jehovah's Witnesses—are so successful at winning converts; despite their absurd beliefs, they are proud to promote them.

Why does evangelism have to be personal? It's obvious, when you think about it. You can't convert a nation, much less "the culture," because nations and cultures don't convert. Nations can't accept Christ into their hearts. Cultures can't be baptized in the name of the Father, and of the Son, and of the Holy Spirit. Only people can.

True, after Constantine accepted the Faith, Rome quickly followed. But the first Christians weren't trying to convert empires or even emperors. They were hoping to convert men and women—all of them—including the man Constantine.

Remember what Lewis said: "The Christians who did most for the present world were just those who thought most of the next." The Fathers of the Church weren't trying to save humanity: they were trying to save humans, one by one. They were deeply, personally invested in the eternal fate of every soul they encountered.

That's what it really means to love your neighbor, and this love, in turn, gave credence to the Creed. Great men like Constantine became Christian because Christians didn't care about "great men."

In the year 258, the emperor Valerian went to Saint Lawrence and demanded that he surrender all the Church's treasures to the government. Three days later, Lawrence arrived at the imperial palace leading a crowd of beggars, lepers, orphans, and widows. "Here are the treasures of the Church" he announced, "and she is much richer than any emperor."

Valerian, as we said, promptly burned Lawrence alive. But it was this pure, reckless, undiscerning love that won the heart of his heir fifty-four years later.

Today, "real Christians" are reluctant to go into the streets and proclaim the Good News of the risen Christ. We don't want to be ignored or mocked. We don't want to be cornered by some old woman talking about how she used to pray the Rosary every day, until her grandson was killed in Iraq. We don't want to listen to a drug addict drone on about how she overdosed on heroin last year and saw an angel. It all seems a little pointless.

But this is a lie, straight from the Father of Lies. And it's even more ingenious because it's a threefold lie.

First, we convince ourselves that our efforts probably don't matter. Then we tell ourselves that, anyway, most people are broken in a way that we're not—so maybe they don't matter, or maybe we can't reach them even if they do. Finally, we convince ourselves that there's a vast sea of unbroken people out there who can be converted with a pamphlet or a YouTube video or a clever turn of phrase—so we don't need to enter into their personality, their humanity, their brokenness. We take a pass on the hard cases (which are everywhere) because we're always looking for the easy jobs (which are nowhere, and never have been).

The first Christians had none of these hang-ups. The Lord commands us: "Go into all the world and preach the gospel to every creature" and "make disciples of all the nations." That's exactly what the first Christians did, with a total disregard for worldly wisdom.

The explosive growth of the Early Church may seem miraculous. And, in a sense, it was: the early Christians—miraculously—devoted their lives to something wild and true! Yet the sociologist Rodney Stark estimates that Christianity's rate of growth between the death of Jesus and the conversion of Constantine was roughly equivalent to the Mormon Church's growth-rate during the nineteenth century. Hard work pays off, whether it's done to further God's kingdom, or a worldly one, or any other cause.

Traditional Christians—Catholic, Orthodox, and Protestant—envy the gains that are made by false sects. And yet those sects are simply obeying the Great Commission. They're following the example of the Church Fathers. Why are we so afraid to do the same?

Christians usually say that the Church was born on the first Pentecost. After Christ's death, His Apostles had been hiding in the upper room. They had even *seen* the risen Lord and been given the Great Commission. But they lacked the *grace* to act—which finally came to them on the tenth day after Jesus ascended into Heaven. The Master called down the Holy Ghost on His friends like tongues of fire, and their souls ignited.

We all know what happens next. At once, Peter went into the street, preaching the Good News. "Be saved from this perverse generation" he cried. As the Book of Acts tells us, "Those who gladly received his word were baptized; and that day about three thousand souls were added to them" (2:40, 41).

This is the power of the Holy Ghost working through willing men and willing women of fasting and prayer. Christ has promised us that His Spirit will abide with us forever. Those tongues of fire still hover over each and every one of us, each and every day. The Lord gives us all the grace we need to conquer the world, and then some. All we have to do is let ourselves catch fire.

As with all the Works of Mercy, though, each Christian must take *personal responsibility* for the Church's apostolic mission. As Pope Francis wrote in his prophetic apostolic exhortation *Evangelii Gaudium*,

> In virtue of their baptism, all the members of the People of God have become missionary disciples. All the baptized, whatever their position in the Church, or their level of instruction in the faith, are agents of evangelization, and it would be insufficient to envisage a plan of evangelization to be carried out by professionals while the rest of the faithful would simply be passive recipients.

Evangelism, like prayer, fasting, and the other Works of Mercy, is a universal vocation. We all must embrace the apostolic life, the layman no less than the friar. If we're ever going to rebuild Christendom, we must feel the Great Commission charged to us *personally* by the Master.

But let's say you devote three hours a week to street evangelism. Let's say you keep at it for ten years. And let's say that not a single person you speak to ever turns up at church on Sunday. Were you just wasting your Saturdays? No. Absolutely not.

First of all, you've made a heroic effort to obey Jesus's command. And that will make Him very happy.

Secondly, you have no idea how He's going to work through your encounter with the people you meet. I once came across two women smoking crack behind a dumpster near the public library. They looked at me side-eyed as I walked up to them. I have no idea what they were expecting me to say. But all I did was offer them some food and a rosary. Their eyes filled with tears. "No one ever talks to us," one of them said.

Another time, I gave a bottle of water and a rosary to a young woman who passed our group's table in the park. She, too, started to cry. "I left my boyfriend last night," she said. "He beat me. I took my son and drove away. I left everything." She gave me a hug and said, "God sent you to me today. You're my angel."

I'm not trying to boast. I've got nothing to brag about. This is all ridiculously simple. You can do it too—and I find it very hard. Most folks you meet aren't going to fall at your feet and ask you to teach them the one true faith. (That did happen to me once, but when I told the young woman that we don't become angels when we die, she lost interest.) God, however, is love. And when you love your neighbor, you bring him closer to God.

Thirdly, you develop a habit of evangelization. Stark also points out that new religious movements generally spread through kinship networks. This was true of Christianity in ancient Rome; it's equally true of Mormonism in modern America. But what's interesting is that groups that succeed in winning converts through kinship networks *also* evangelize strangers. I'm not sure why that is, but I have a pretty good guess.

When we try to share our Faith with our friends and family, there's a temptation to find the right "angle." We want to show how Christianity is most relevant to their "lived experience." But this means that we're not really *evangelizing* them at all. We're not sharing the Good News of Jesus Christ. We're not facilitating a personal encounter with the risen Lord. We're trying to fix some specific problem in their lives. We're trying to use "persuasive words of human wisdom," which Saint Paul warned us against, rather than a "demonstration of the Spirit" — and so our faith seems grounded more in the wisdom of men than in the power of God (see 1 Cor. 2:1–5).

Evangelism means fostering a relationship, not just telling someone what to think or how to live. If liturgy is setting aside time for the love of God, then evangelism is setting aside time for the love of man. Evangelism is the highest form of charity because God is the greatest good. If we give someone God, we give him (literally) everything.

Of course, we do not actually *give* someone God. We cannot convert anyone. Only God can do that. Our God, in His infinite kindness, calls us to serve as missionaries for our own benefit. He, the great *Philanthropos* — the Lover of Mankind — doesn't need a wingman. But He lets us play the part anyway.

The beauty of street evangelism is that we have no choice but to fall back on the *kerygma* — the essentials of our Faith. We're stuck with the elevator pitch: that God so loved the world that He gave His only begotten Son, that whosoever believeth in Him should not perish but have everlasting life. Once we witness the power of the Christian *kerygma*, our own vain attempts to "apply" the Gospel to our friends' and families' lives quickly start to look ridiculous. Because they are.

I gave evangelism its own chapter because it's not mentioned in my list from the Book of Tobit. But evangelism isn't distinct from fasting, prayer, almsgiving, and righteousness. The five of them are inseparable. In fact, the most powerful link may be the least obvious—to wit, the link between evangelism and prayer.

According to the Fathers, the end of all prayer is *theosis*. Theosis is the process by which human beings become "partakers of the divine nature," as Saint Peter puts it. Likewise, we know that the true evangelist is one who leads his neighbor to a direct, personal encounter with the living God. The more we pray, the deeper we enter into God's nature; the deeper we enter into God's nature, the more we can *be* His presence in the lives of our fellow man.

This is why Saint Peter had such great success on the first Pentecost. *He* wasn't preaching to the masses. Rather, it was the Holy Spirit dwelling *in* him and speaking *through* him. This is also why so many of the great saints—like Christ Himself—drew men to God by their mere presence. Saint Francis of Assisi probably didn't say, "Preach the gospel at all times; when necessary, use words." But it's exactly right, and he said it without words.

St. Seraphim of Sarov, I think, may have put it even better: "Acquire the Spirit of Peace, and thousands around you will be saved." Before we can become missionaries, we must become mystics; and once we become mystics, we can't help but become missionaries. In fact, we become *theophanies*: manifestations of God in the world.

Still, I wonder how many of us would recognize Christ if we saw Him?

7

How Beauty Will Save the World

*I shall bless her hunts with blessings, I shall satisfy
her poor with bread. With salvation I shall clothe
her priests, her saints shall exult with joy.*

—Psalm 131:15–16

*It is only as joy that the Church was victorious in the
world, and it lost the world when it lost that joy.*

—Father Alexander Schmemann

There's a certain trend among conservative Christians that's been gnawing at me for a few years now. I don't know how to describe it, except that they're really down on being *nice*. It's not that they're in favor of being mean; at least, that's not how they would put it. But they're absolutely emphatic that being "nice" is not a virtue.

For example, a few years ago, right-wing Catholic media was in a tizzy about something they called the "Church of Nice." Mostly they meant those social-climbing bishops who water down the Faith in order to spare non-Catholics' feelings and ingratiate themselves to our post-Christian society. But this tendency exists among the intelligentsia as well. These folks will point out that many great Catholic minds were huge jerks. Look at St. Jerome! Look at Evelyn Waugh! Look at ... well, those are the only two examples I ever hear.

It's not only Catholics, though. Around the same time that Catholic media was railing against the "Church of Nice," Protestants were revolting against the "winsome" evangelism of Tim Keller (memory eternal!). They argued that Keller's aversion to politics — his refusal to involve himself in the "Culture War" — was an abdication of his duties both as pastor and theologian. The implication is that Christians have a duty to embrace the "conservative" elements of our Faith, even if it displeases our post-Christian neighbors.

I had thought the anti-nice movement had begun to die down. Then, in March of this year, *The Lamp*, that venerable rag, published an essay by Robert Wyllie called "Against Humanity."

"I do not wish to criticize human beings," Dr. Wyllie explains, "some of whom I assume are good people. When I argue 'against humanity,' it is to detonate the first denotation in *Webster's Dictionary*: the quality of being humane. It is this humanity—amiability, mild benevolence, easygoing kindness, what now passes for basic human decency—to which I feel compelled to object."

Dr. Wyllie rebukes Charles Dickens, for example, because *A Christmas Carol* makes no mention of the Incarnation and "offers sentiment rather than policy" in regard to the suffering of the poor. By the end, he has accused liberals (broadly defined) of the same error. "Liberals," he writes, "sacrifice principle and policy to clutch the pearls of humanity."

Well, let's say this about that.

First of all, Dickens offers a bit more than mere sentiment. At the end of the story, the Ghost of Christmas Future shows Scrooge a vision of his own grave. Moved by this *memento mori* to a contemplation of the Last Things, he gives Bob Cratchit a raise, allowing him to pay for the surgery or medicine needed to save Tiny Tim's life.

Paying one's employees a decent salary so they can afford health care seems like pretty sound policy to me. But I know there's a certain kind of socialist who gets angry when the rich are benevolent toward the poor—just as there's a certain kind of capitalist who gets angry when government programs do what they're supposed to. That's not charity, though. It's not justice. It's ideology.

Secondly, does anyone think that we as a society suffer from a glut of amiability? Is our civilization being crushed beneath the weight of our mild benevolence? When you go out in public—to work, or study, or shop, or whatever—are you suffocated by strangers' easy kindness?

Thirdly—and most importantly—"niceness" is an integral part of the ordinary praxis of the Christian faith. St. Paul himself commands the Ephesians to "be kind to one another, tenderhearted, forgiving one another, even as God in Christ forgave you." Likewise, he tells the Colossians: "As the elect of God, holy and beloved, put on tender mercies, kindness, humility, meekness, longsuffering, bearing with one another, and forgiving one another, if anyone has a complaint against another; even as Christ forgave you, so you also must do."

For the first Christians, this wasn't a throwaway line. On the contrary, they viewed it as central to the daily practice of Christianity. This fact has been attested to by experts everywhere, from Tertullian to Rodney Stark. As the former famously said, "It is our care of the helpless, our practice of loving kindness that brands us in the eyes of many of our opponents. 'Only look,' they say, 'look how they love one another!'" Nor was their loving-kindness limited to fellow believers. Remember how our old friend Julian the Apostate complained to his fellow pagans, "The impious Galileans support not only their poor, but ours as well."

In fact, scholars from Stark to Tom Holland to David Bentley Hart have argued that the first Christians' kindness—their selflessness, their decency, their attentiveness to the needs of their fellow man—was central to the spread of our Faith. Tim Keller was absolutely right: "winsomeness" is essential to evangelism. We're naturally attracted to those who take an interest in our good.

It's true, as some might point out, that the psalm also says, "Let the righteous strike me; It shall be a kindness." This is why the Roman Church lists *rebuking the sinner* among her Spiritual Works of Mercy. True kindness—true charity—sometimes means confronting our loved ones about some grave sin and helping them to repent. But, again, this is not the *ordinary* expression of kindness.

Of course, you encounter sinners every time you walk out the door, or glance at your phone, or look in the mirror. But correcting them isn't always the right thing to do. The Fathers say we must consider whether, by rebuking the sinner, we may not drive him deeper into sin. To quote St. Augustine: "Perhaps from shame he might begin to defend his sin; and him whom you thought to make a better man, you make worse." (See: *Westboro Baptist Church*.)

According to the Fathers, we should rebuke only someone we're very close to—a close friend or family member. This person should know that we love him and that we desire his good. He should trust our judgment. And if and when we do rebuke him, we should do so privately, and in the gentlest possible terms. In other words, we have to be very nice to someone for a very long time before we can justify rebuking him for his sins—and even then, we must do it nicely.

It's also true that, sometimes, only rudeness can awaken us from our ego-sleep. Athonite monks have perfected the art of softening people's hearts by insulting them. But unless you spend twelve hours a day in prayer, I'd stick to more conventional methods; for the most part, someone's more likely to agree with your ideas—or convert to your religion—if you're nice to him. That's not even Psychology 101; it's too obvious to mention.

Why, then, are these polemics against "niceness" so popular today? Why are they so common especially among "conservative" Christians, who pride themselves on their doctrinal purity and fidelity to Church tradition? Why do they so proudly announce that "being 'nice' isn't a virtue" when it clearly is?

Partly, I think, it comes down to the fact that most conservative Christians don't know their faith nearly as well as they think they do. Or, rather, they assume that whatever they've labeled "conservative" is compatible with—if not derived from—Christianity. Like progressive Christians, they've inherited their values from secular ideologies. Their phronema is not formed by Scripture and the Church Fathers, but by . . . something else. *Anything* else.

Not to keep picking on Dr. Wyllie, but he also mocks Dickens's "philanthropic dream." As I said, one of the titles of God used in the Eastern Church is "lover of mankind"—in Greek, *philanthropos.* This is from the Divine Liturgy of Saint John Chrysostom. It doesn't get much more traditional than that.

Clearly, "niceness" is not something that infected the Church from the outside. It's one of Christianity's great gifts to Western civilization. True: as our society becomes unchurched, much of the traditional theological context of our Christian values is stripped away. The values themselves, which were once fundamental to our social order, have become watered down or perverted. And niceness is one of them. But attacking "humanity" because it's abused by secular liberals is like saying that the problem with gay marriage is *marriage.*

To put it another way, Flannery O'Connor famously said:

> If other ages felt less, they saw more, even though they saw with the blind, prophetical, unsentimental eye of acceptance, which is to say, of faith. In the absence of this faith now, we govern by tenderness. It is a tenderness which, long cut off from the person of Christ, is wrapped in theory. When tenderness is detached from the source of tenderness, its logical outcome is terror. It ends in forced-labor camps and in the fumes of the gas chamber.

She's right, of course. And Christians naturally—rightly—want to offer a counter-witness to this fake tenderness. But the opposite of fake tenderness is not real harshness, cruelty, and so on. It's real tenderness. And that's exactly what Christ offers.

It also comes down to plain-old sin. We all know why progressive Christians explain away the story of Sodom and Gomorrah: they like sodomy. By the same token, conservative Christians "debunk" the "Church of Nice" because they want to be mean. At the very least, they want an excuse *not* to be kind, tenderhearted, and so forth. They're making excuses for their sin. It's exactly the same thing, and anyone who disagrees is a sophist.

To be clear, I agree that insults are sometimes useful for snapping people out of their sinful slumber. There's a story about Saint Paisios the Athonite confronting a pornographer who visited his Mount Athos to "debunk" this wonder-working monk:

> When they [the pornographer and his companions] arrived, the elder received them in his yard, saying, "Sit down and let me serve you something." The elder served the other two gentlemen first, and then stood in front of the first man and turned the plate upside down, letting the sweet fall in the mud.
>
> "I dropped it," he said, "but that doesn't matter. Pick it up and eat it anyway."
>
> The fellow was insulted: "How do you expect me to eat it when it's filthy?"
>
> The elder sternly replied, "And why do you give people filth to eat?"
>
> Stunned, embarrassed, and in some fear, the man got up and left, but he went back again the next day and spoke with the elder. He told me he felt then as though the ground were shifting under his feet. The conversation was brief.
>
> "What am I supposed to do?" he asked.
>
> The elder responded, "First of all, shut down your business, then come back and talk to me again."

He returned to Thessaloniki, closed the business, and began to look for new work. After about a month, he went to speak with Saint Paisios, who told him to go to Confession and taught him to put his life in order spiritually.

This is a great example of how giving offense is *actually* a salutary thing to do.

And of course, Our Lord Himself could be quite stinging. For instance, I remember when a certain Jesuit agitator declared, "Calling people animals is sinful." The Twitters were quick to point out that Jesus called the Pharisees as a brood of vipers and referred to the Canaanites as dogs. So, why can't we?

Truth be told, I'm not a huge fan of this particular Jesuit. And he definitely overstated his case. Still, I think it's good to remind ourselves periodically of the first rule of Scriptural exegesis: *You are not Jesus.* Whenever you read a story about Jesus's life, you should not identify with Jesus. You should identify with the sinner whom He is healing, converting, forgiving, upbraiding, flagellating, or what have you.

Again, I'm not saying that Elder Paisios did anything wrong. I'm not deying that, in God's hands, a cruel word may be used break a heart of stone. The point, rather, is this: *Only rarely does insulting someone lead to that person's conversion or repentance, and only the holiest of men are capable of discerning such occasions.* Jesus can do it. Paisios can do it. But if you or I try to insult someone into holiness, we're probably going to have the opposite effect.

By the way, this isn't only a problem for "the Right." Whenever a traditional Christian defends some point of traditional Christian morality, you'll hear one of our lefty friends cry, "I thought Jesus ate with prostitutes and tax collectors!" Once again, the proper response is: *Do you identify with Jesus in that parable?*

This is where liberal Christianity becomes—ironically; hilariously—elitist. Sorry, folks, but God's not saying you must condescend to eat with sinners. No: *you* are the sinner. *He* condescends to eat with *you*.

As for us recovering sinners (i.e., Christians), Saint Paul gives us a different rule: "But now I have written to you not to keep company with anyone named a brother, who is sexually immoral, or covetous, or an idolater, or a reviler, or a drunkard, or an extortioner—not even to eat with such a person" (1 Cor. 5:11). Why? Because, not being Jesus, you can't trust yourself not to fall into that person's vice.

Of course, rules are meant to be broken.

Early in the seventh century, there lived a monk named Vitalis. He was born in Gaza, but he spent most of his life in the monastery of Seridus in Alexandria.

Every day, Vitalis worked as a common laborer. Every night, he would visit the home of a different prostitute and pay her his earnings. "I beg you," he would say, "take this money and do not sin with anyone tonight." He would then spend the night at her home, praying and reading the psalms while she slept. He asked only that they not reveal the purpose of his visit.

As you might expect, Vitalis was judged constantly—by townspeople, by priests, even by his fellow monks. But for the sake of holy humility, Vitalis continued to do his good works in secret. Only after his death did the Gazan sex-worker community begin speaking of the monk's charity, chastity, and humility.

Saint Vitalis of Gaza is a beautiful soul who lived a beautiful life. Remember, though: he's a saint. If an ordinary Christian man (me, for example) spent every night with a different prostitute, his story wouldn't have such a happy ending.

If you'll allow me to make a gross generalization, it seems to me that the Western mind is addicted to gross generalizations. It can deal only in absolutes, especially where morality is concerned. We say, "Either it's okay to insult people for their own good, or it's not.

And Jesus insulted people for their own good. Therefore, so can I." Or, "Either it's okay to hang out with grave and unrepentant sinners, or it's not. And Jesus was friends with grave, unrepentant sinners. Therefore, I can be, too."

To be clear, these aren't just bad answers. They're bad answers to bad questions. The whole premise is faulty.

When in doubt, just remember: *you are not Jesus*. You're probably not Paisios of Mount Athos or Vitalis of Gaza either. Of course, we should strive to be like them. Of course. We should fast, pray, and give alms until we become so virtuous, peaceful, and charitable that we can exercise holy prudence in following or applying the moral law, for the sake of leading others to Christ (see: *oikonomia*). Absolutely. No arguments here.

But I'm not there yet. And statistically speaking, you're probably not either. No offense, dear reader! It's just that living saints are few and far between these days.

The good news is that, if we do become holy, we will rarely (if ever) need to be harsh. As Saint John Chrysostom said, "Holiness of life is better than a thousand sermons." And our exemplar in this, of course, is Christ Himself. I think David Bentley Hart puts it best. "Christ is a persuasion," he says, "a form evoking desire":

> What Christian thought offers the world is not a set of "rational" arguments that (suppressing certain of their premises) force assent from others by leaving them, like the interlocutors of Socrates, at a loss for words; rather, it stands before the world principally with the story it tells concerning God and creation, the form of Christ, the loveliness of the practice of Christian charity.

For Christ "embodies a real and imitable practice, a style of being that conforms to the beauty of divine love, but that is also a way of worldly godliness." Professor Hart uses the word *beauty* with great care. In the Christian tradition, *beauty* isn't just another word for *prettiness*. It's *a way of knowing God*. This is why a man can have a deep, lasting conversion after encountering a French cathedral, or a Greek icon, or an Anglican hymn. Beauty is the language of God. It's the thumbprint of the Creator.

And what's true of beautiful art is also true of beautiful lives. When we read about saints such as Francis (or Anthony of the Desert, or Augustine, or Mother Teresa) we find them compelling, in exactly the same way we find the cathedral or the icon or the hymn compelling. They validate, and explicate, the Faith. They draw us into the Church. They make us want to be part of their "thing," whatever glorious, miraculous "thing" makes possible such sights, such sounds, such men and women. They don't convince us of Christianity on an intellectual level. They bypass the rational-critical parts of our brains and pour into our hearts.

Take another example. Think of how many people convert to Christianity under the influence of folks such as C. S. Lewis and G. K. Chesterton. The younger of the two died more than sixty years ago, and yet both still help to win hundreds (if not thousands) of souls every year. And why is that? They're brilliant, of course. But their writing is also *beautiful*, in the way Saint John's writings are beautiful. There's a warmth, a kindliness, a good humor that we find irresistible. Lewis and Chesterton clearly love what they're writing about, and whom they're writing to, i.e., you and me.

Even a hardened atheist feels that a debate with men like these would be enjoyable. And he feels sure that, if he could sit down with Lewis or Chesterton, Lewis or Chesterton would take him seriously. Neither would try to "sell" the Faith, either by shoving it down someone's throat or by watering it down. Lewis and Chesterton would just be a couple of friends shooting the breeze down at the pub. By the second round, we're secretly hoping they'll win.[8]

Or take the novels of J. R. R. Tolkien. If you spend any time around thoughtful Christians, you'll meet at least one person who converted after reading *The Lord of the Rings*. Such people will say that Tolkien's heroes seemed truly good, and his villains truly evil, in a way they'd never encountered in another book. Middle Earth seems real in a way that Hogwarts and Westeros never could.

Tolkien rejected the idea that he was a Catholic novelist—that is, an author of Catholic novels. He believed that good literature couldn't be sectarian. Yet no one can deny that his writings are defined by a deeply Christian moral order. They're animated by a thoroughly Catholic vision of *sacramentality*. That's why countless men, women, and children have gone to his books looking for a light read and have come away with the true Faith.

That's what beauty is. That's what it does. And that's why Dostoyevsky said it will save the world. Polemics and apologetics have their place. They speak to the mind and tell it what's true. But beauty knocks at the door of the heart—and the door must be opened before truth can make its case.

A life of holiness, simplicity, and joy is the most beautiful thing of all. It's the most persuasive argument ever devised. Use it liberally.

---

[8]   I wonder if the prostitutes and tax collectors felt the same way during their lunches with the Master.

8

Enchantment
and Its Enemies

As dreams are to one awake, so, O Lord,
thou shalt in thy city turn their idols to nothing.

—Psalm 72:20

Sorcery and sanctity, these are the only realities.

—Arthur Machen

W hat do Thomas Edison, Oscar Wilde, Mahatma Gandhi, Gustav Mahler, D. T. Suzuki, and Vice President Henry Wallace have in common? All were deeply involved in Theosophy.

For those who don't know, Theosophy is one of the oldest and most successful New Age cults. It was founded in the 1870s as a spin-off of spiritualism. Like spiritualists of the old-school, Theosophists hold seances, complete with crystal balls and moving tables. However, while spiritualists attempt to contact the dead, Theosophists try to communicate with a vast hierarchy of ancient gurus, called "Ascended Masters," who deliver occult teachings through automatic writing.

To modern ears, this all sounds ridiculous.[9] But to men of the late-nineteenth and early-twentieth centuries, Theosophy wasn't a religion. It was a science. Each new day seemed to bring a revolution in man's understanding of the world—and of himself. New studies on energy, particularly electricity and its relationship to the human brain, led many to believe that the soul was not necessarily

___

[9] Madame Blavatsky claimed to correspond with a Hindu "Master" with the unlikely name of Hoot Koomi. He's not to be mistaken for Koot Hoomi *Singh*, the Sikh "Master" with whom she also communed.

a supernatural phenomenon but that some kind of life (or at least consciousness) beyond death was possible—even probable!—in purely natural terms.

Again, to us in the twenty-first century, it seems as if these folks were drawing gigantic conclusions from a very small body of new information. Granted, that information was *very* new. But in hindsight, we can see clearly that the Theosophists and spiritualists simply got carried away.

Now, I want you to think about this phenomenon whenever you hear someone say that our universe is a gigantic computer simulation (i.e., *simulation hypothesis*) or that artificial intelligence will eventually evolve into God—not *a* god, but *the* God. These theories are believed by countless members of our modern elite, from Elon Musk to Neil deGrasse Tyson.

And that's not surprising. Strangely enough, this stems from humanity's deeply conservative nature. We are herd animals. We are conditioned by our environment, especially by the people around us. When we discover something new and shiny, we get excited, and that excitement quickly spreads throughout the herd. Soon enough, our individual and collective lives revolve around the Shiny New Thing. It becomes like a God to us. In many instances, it actually becomes our God: the bedrock of our entire metaphysical system, our whole worldview. And the rise of a new religion—obviously it tells the rise of a new priestly or prophetic class. Whether they realize it or not, men like Edison and Musk are incentivized to exaggerate the importance of their inventions or products—no matter how important those inventions or products may be in real life. It gives them greater prestige, greater authority, greater wealth, greater power.

Christians need to bear this truth closely in mind whenever some new technology or scientific discovery appears to debunk our Faith. This was said about the discovery of the heliocentric universe. It's what others said about the discovery of evolution. It's what still others said about those incredible scientific leaps that took place in the late-nineteenth century. And, of course, the same thing could be said about Internet technology and artificial intelligence. Yet as these so-called solutions multiply, so do the questions they pose. The cosmos is infinitely more complicated than Thales ever imagined. The more we learn about the universe, the more mysterious it becomes.

Of course, that's not proof positive of Christianity. But it's certainly not proof negative—no matter what the pop atheists claim.

We should also consider very carefully how living in a "post-Christian" society affects not only *what* we believe but also *how* we believe.

For instance, last winter I was helping a friend stack firewood when he told me that he had been having doubts about his faith. We talked about it for a while, but I quickly realized that I was in over my head. So I asked him, "Have you spoken to your priest?" He looked at me sadly and said, "I don't want to make him doubt too."

Doubt is nothing new, of course. The Psalmist says, "The fool says in his heart there is no God." But the *internalized materialism* that powers contemporary forms of doubt seems to me quintessentially modern. The prevailing atheistic worldview is so prevalent, we feel pressured to think we're deluding ourselves; and we almost take it for granted that our fellow Christians are deluding *themselves* too. It's not innocence but the ceremony of innocence. And should anyone break the fourth wall, the curtain will come down. The ceremony will be drowned.

Before the dawn of the twentieth century, virtually all cultures, everywhere in the world, were religious, in the broad sense of the term. Whether they were animists (like the Native Americans), shamanists (like the Aboriginal Australians), polytheists (like the ancient Greeks), or dualists (like the ancient Persians), they were all "theistic" by default. They took it for granted that there were beings and powers that couldn't be explained simply in terms of matter and energy. They were confident of the existence of non-physical as well as physical things.

There were gods, of course: the creators and masters of the universe. But most humans sensed the presence of lesser forces in the world: powers, intelligences, that live and work and play all around us and yet (for the most part) go unseen.

The Romans called these forces "minor gods," and, boy, were there a lot of them. There was a god for everything in ancient Rome, and sometimes more than one. According to Saint Augustine, a small army of them were supposed to have tagged along with newlyweds on their honeymoon. "When a male and a female are united, the god Jugatinus presides," he wrote. "Well, let this be borne with. But the married woman must be brought home: the god Domidicus also is invoked. That she may remain with her husband, the goddess Manturnæ is used."

"Why is the bedchamber filled with a crowd of deities, when even the groomsmen have departed?" Augustine asks. Which is a fair question.

In Wales, you'll find the *Tylwyth Teg*: the Fair Family, also known as fairies. The Norse called them *landvaettir*, "heath wights," or nature spirits. In Arabia, they're called *djinn*, or genies.

By the way, the *djinn* aren't huge blue things that grant wishes. They're just invisible creatures, children of Allah, like humans. They have moral agency; some are good, some are bad, and some are just mischievous. They're religious, too. Mohammed devotes a whole chapter of the Qur'an to these creatures.

In surah 72, Mohammed says that God revealed that the *djinn* have been listening to him preach. "Indeed, we have heard a wondrous recitation," the genies say. "Now we believe that our Lord, Exalted is His Majesty, has never taken a mate nor offspring, and that the foolish of us used to utter outrageous falsehoods about Allah."

The *djinn*, like the Fair Family and the heath wights, are a race unto themselves. They are not ghosts—though in some cultures, the Unseen is a mixture of elemental creatures and disembodied human souls. The Japanese, for instance, have *kami*. They are like the souls of nature. They are like the Roman gods. Everything has a *kami*: rice, the sun, you name it. And because Shinto makes no distinction between nature and supernature, its faithful believe that the souls of their ancestors may continue to dwell in the world after death (disembodied *kami*, so to speak).

This belief in the unseen isn't quite the same as theism or religiosity. Let's call it *supernaturalism*. And, in many ways, supernaturalism is more fundamental to the human experience than religion. It's why old Yankees have remained deeply superstitious long after they abandoned Puritanism. Religion (as we use the term) is a matter of theology, mythology, and ceremony. Supernaturalism is a matter of empirical fact.

Or, at least, it was.

Once upon a time, in Christendom, every facet of human society was ordered toward revealing the imprint of the Divine. Even the king was an officer of the Church, sworn to uphold the Faith within his realm. Workers were given time off for baptisms, funerals, weddings, and major feasts. Music was sacred. Art was sacred art. Church spires soared over every skyline. Bells rang out in every town and village across Europe. Schools were run by monks and hospitals by friars.

While the Christianity of the Middle Ages may have been especially intense, "an amorous dream of Heaven," as Maeztu called it, the form it followed was pretty much the norm for all premodern civilizations. Worship and prayer are always the heart of public life. (That's why *cult*, or *cultus*, is the root of the word *culture*.) No doubt some individuals believed more strongly than others. And there have always been heretics of one sort or another. Still, just about everyone *believed*.

Today, our society—our culture—is ordered toward atheistic materialism, and accordingly it instills materialist convictions in its citizens. All the major institutions of our public life—political, economic, and cultural—encourage us to suppress, deny, or mock our "supernaturalist" instincts. We're trained, almost from birth, to dismiss phenomena that can't be explained in terms of matter and energy. The only spirituality we tolerate is the sort you can buy in a Hallmark store: scented candles and inspirational quotes.

This is what I mean by "internalized materialism." However we come to the Faith, whether through reason or beauty or some miraculous road-to-Emmaus moment, we'll spend our whole lives struggling against a deep cultural skepticism. It is almost impossible to shake the idea that not only Christianity but *any* supernaturalist account of reality is slightly ridiculous. Deep down, we'll always wonder if the universe is nothing but "rust and stardust."

Another word for "internalized materialism" is *disenchantment*, a word that is considerably older and has a more distinguished pedigree. It arose from the writings of Schiller and Weber, and has been explored by all the greatest thinkers of our time: Charles Taylor, Rowan Williams, John Milbank, Rod Dreher, David Bentley Hart, D. C. Schindler, Iain McGilchrist, Jordan Peterson, Paul Kingsnorth, Martin Shaw, and Jonathan Pageau, to name just a few.

I am anti-disenchantment, for reasons that should be clear by now. But I'm also wary of the usual remedy: "re-enchantment." During the Catholic Church's "Synod on Synodality," in an article in the *National Catholic Reporter*, a Jesuit regent named Patrick Saint-Jean urged the synod to embrace voodoo. Dr. Saint-Jean (who is Haitian) says of his enslaved forefathers:

> For them, this ancestral spiritual practice was a doorway to meet Christ. Vodou was a way to come to gather, to pray, discern and open themselves to the work of the Holy Spirit. This was their culture and spiritual avenue where they encountered the Spirit.
>
> Like many other local spiritual systems, Vodou appeals to many who take shelter in the margin of the Gospel. This helps to connect them with all spiritual possibilities, including how people speak, eat, and pray, as a way to connect with the Divine.

Many Westerners, and not a few Haitians, believe that voodoo is evil. Not true, according to Dr. Saint-Jean. Rather, it was "misunderstood by the Eurocentric mind of the enslavers," who then "forced their enslaved to undermine their own spiritual practice." In fact, voodoo is fully compatible with Christianity.

Dr. Saint-Jean goes on to explain: "This synod in Rome will be a new way for us to challenge the lack of spiritual imagination that was inculcated in us" by white slave traders and so forth. And if you feel inclined to point out that the Catholic Church explicitly teaches that magic in all its forms is demonic—well, don't. "We ought to believe in the possibility of everything from the Holy Spirit," says Dr. Saint-Jean.

Now, let's get the obvious points out of the way first. Voodoo is not compatible with Christianity. It incorporates both sorcery and idolatry, both of which are forbidden, completely and un-ambiguously, by all of Scripture and Tradition. Indeed, certain voodoo spells, known as *juju*, are designed to harm or even kill other people. In Africa, for instance, human traffickers use juju to intimidate their sex slaves, threatening to curse their victims and their families if they try to escape or alert the authorities.

Even if spells were intended to work good, the Church makes no distinction between (benevolent) "white magic" and (malevo-lent) "black magic." Whether you're trying to kill an ex-lover or bring about good weather, it doesn't matter. Sorcery and idolatry, in all their forms, are categorically forbidden by the Christian faith.

And in case you were wondering, race has nothing to do with it. The European Christians undoubtedly tried to suppress the practice of voodoo among their slaves. But these Christians also tried to suppress the practice of voodoo among their fellow Euro-peans. At the height of the Atlantic slave trade, Protestants from New England to Germany were embroiled in their infamous "witch trials." And just a few generations before, the Catholic Church had fought against hermetic and alchemical magic, which came into vogue during the Renaissance.

So, this has nothing to do with race or class or creed or sect. The simple fact is that Christianity and magic are incompatible. Period. Full stop.

Dr. Saint-Jean's article calls to mind a series of essays that ap-peared earlier in 2023 in the *European Conservative*. Their author, an academic named Sebastian Morello, asks: "Can Hermetic Magic Rescue the Church?" He answers his own question over the course of three articles, but let's skip to the conclusion:

> I declare that Christ alone can rescue His Church, but we have ousted Him in a diabolic effort to divorce Bride from

Bridegroom. We have lost the primacy of the supernatural: however much the Lord may seek to rescue His Church from its current trajectory of self-destruction, He finds a Church whose members largely don't believe they need rescuing. They are under a spell, and that spell must be broken. Perhaps the sacred magic of Hermes Trismegistus is what's needed to banish the black magic of Enlightened man. And thereby, we may begin to retrieve *meaning*, and in turn start the Church's process of humbling itself before the true King of the Universe.

If you're surprised to find a right-wing, Christian magazine giving space to sorcerers, you haven't been paying attention.

Conservatives have always had a soft spot for certain kinds of magicians. Éliphas Lévi, the father of French occultism, was a man of the Right. He was an outspoken disciple of the royalist philosopher Joseph de Maistre. Lévi believed that occultism was the perfect antidote to the bland, leveling secularism of the modern West. The poet W. B. Yeats[10] was also both a conservative (a supporter of Mussolini, no less!) and a practitioner of Hermetic magic.

Today, many of the alt-right are disciples of Julius Evola. Evola is best known for his book *Revolt Against the Modern World*. He called his political ideology *imperialismo pagano*, or "pagan imperialism." His thinking was rooted in an idiosyncratic synthesis of Nietzscheanism, Hermeticism, and Indian tantrism.

Dr. Morello (like Evola, Lévi, and the others) is, avowedly, a man of the Right. And I think it's fair to say that Patrick Saint-Jean is a man of the Left. Yet both identify the same malaise afflicting the Western world. After all, when Dr. Saint-Jean refers to

---

[10] My all-time favorite.

Europeans' "lack of spiritual imagination," he's basically talking about disenchantment.

The pagan Right and the pagan Left both blame the other's "side" for stealing modernity's soul. But more importantly: *neither believes that Christianity possesses the necessary tools to heal that malaise.* As a result, both feel the need to reach outside the Christian tradition for answers; and both settle on magic as the solution.

These are just two examples of the rising popularity of witchcraft here in the West. They're striking because they involve professed Christians. But anyone who follows the news will know that sorcery is enjoying a kind of renaissance in the West not seen since … well, the Renaissance. And like the old paganism, it is proving deeply intolerant of "intolerance."

Let's go back to our running example: classical antiquity. The ancient Greeks and Romans were very good at absorbing various religious and ethnic communities into a single polity. They considered this pluralism a mark of their own cultural sophistication.

Yet they also knew that pluralism cuts both ways. If a sect wanted Rome's protection, it had to prove itself. The commitment to Roman pluralism had to supersede belief in the sect's own "exclusivist" dogmas. Over time, Rome devised a standard loyalty test: all citizens were expected to offer a sacrifice to an idol of the god-emperors. As Father John Strickland explains in *The Age of Paradise*,

> The state did not really care what its subjects believed. Rome, as the heir to Hellenic civilization, celebrated religious diversity as part of its pluralistic culture. But a sacrifice to the emperors was proof that whatever convictions one held, he was prepared to accommodate them to the demands of the worldly order.

Just like their forebears, today's pagans are militant relativists. They will not force others to adopt their beliefs, which they only half-believe themselves. But they will condemn Christians who insist that Jesus Christ is the only way, the only truth, the only life.

The pagan Left rejects Christians' prudish morality. The pagan Right scorns their commitment to meekness, humility, and lovingkindness. In other words, both will also accuse the Church of being on the side of slaver. Progressives will say (like Marx) that we're perpetuating racist, homophobic, exploitative power structures grounded in the Crusades, imperialism, and so on. Conservatives, meanwhile, will say (like Nietzsche) that we side with the weak against the strong, the stupid against the intelligent, the inferior against the superior.

Both will make ample room for useful idiots such as Drs. Saint-Jean and Morello, who argue that repaganization will actually be *good* for the Church. But this accommodation won't last for more than a few decades. Eventually, both sides will concoct a loyalty test of their own. Both will demand their "pinch of incense": some gesture, small or large, to prove that our final, ultimate loyalty is to the State, the Party, the Leader—not to Christ.

Given this eventuality, conservatives shouldn't pretend that dechristianization—or, more accurately, repaganization—is just "something that happens to other people." It might be more common on the Left; but the Right is by no means immune. If Christians believe that "conservatism" will shield us from the coming Dark Age, I've got bad news: it won't.

Whatever the future may hold for Western civilization, it will not be a matter of Left versus Right. It will be a matter of Christians versus non-Christians. Neither side of the ideological mainstream will align with Gospel principles. Indeed, large factions within both camps will be hostile to the Church, her teachings, and her faithful.

In addition, a "re-enchanted" West will not necessarily be a re-Christianized West. If anything, the opposite is more likely to be true. Re-enchantment will more likely lead to a more intense anti-Christianity—more intense because, in no small part, the West would be returning to the care of demons.

No one has made this point more clearly, more powerfully, or more compellingly than Blessed Seraphim (Rose) of Platina in his masterpiece, *Orthodoxy and the Future of Religion*.

Seraphim devotes a chapter to each of the New Age movements that gripped America in the late twentieth century, from yoga to the Charismatic Renewal to UFOlogy to neo-paganism. Satan will promote any and all Weltanschauung, for one simple reason: they're not Christian orthodoxy. Some are pseudo-scientific; others are pseudo-religious. But they all serve the Enemy's purposes, because they distract us from the ordinary praxis of Christianity, namely: prayer, fasting, almsgiving, righteousness—and evangelization.

It's especially dangerous when Christians embrace these fads, Seraphim explains, because it poisons the very well of Christianity. Suppose someone grows up in a liberal Protestant sect, or a "Charismatic" Roman Catholic parish. And suppose that spirituality becomes deeply unsatisfying. Is that person going to seek out a community that practices a more traditional, mystical, ascetical form of Christianity? Sometimes, maybe. But statistically speaking, it is far more likely that he will just write off the Faith as tried and failed. There are far more apostates to pseudo-Christianity than there are converts to authentic Christianity.

The Enemy wants only to lure us from the difficult path that leads to the Gate of Life. He doesn't care if we stumble to the Left or to the Right. He doesn't care if we become materialists or magicians. Both suit his purposes nicely. The best thing for us Christians to do—the *only* thing for us Christians to do—is to keep walking that narrow path and to help others to do the same.

This is why Seraphim warns Christians to "walk in the fear of God, trembling lest they lose His grace, which by no means is given to everyone, but only to those who hold the true Faith, lead a life of Christian struggle, and treasure the grace of God which leads them heavenward."

9

Spotless

You who love the Lord, hate evil.

—Psalm 96:10

---

*To be alive is not merely to bear the thought of religion,
to assent to the truth of religion, to wish to be religious;
but to be drawn towards it, to love it,
to delight in it, to obey it.*

—John Henry Newman

In his foreword to *Present Concerns*, Walter Hooper tells a hilarious story about an old Oxford friend of ours:

"Who is Elizabeth Taylor?" asked C. S. Lewis. He and I were talking about the difference between "prettiness" and "beauty," and I suggested that Miss Taylor was a great beauty. "If you read the newspapers," I said to Lewis, "you would know who she is." "Ah-h-h-h!" said Lewis playfully, "but that is how I keep myself 'unspotted from the world.'" He recommended that if I absolutely "must" read newspapers I have a frequent "mouthwash" with *The Lord of the Rings* or some other great book.

Lewis, of course, was quoting the Epistle of Saint James. "Pure and undefiled religion before God and the Father," he wrote, "is this: to visit orphans and widows in their trouble, and to keep oneself unspotted from the world" (1:27). I like this idea, that we have a duty *not* to read the news, for the sake of pure religion. It has saved me a lot of time, a lot of grief, and a lot of money on subscriptions.

I like this story because it changes the way we read that passage from James. At first glance, we might think that keeping "unspotted from the world" means steering clear of its vices. But then slowly we realize it's more than that. It has to do with what Saint

Augustine calls the *ordo amoris*: the ordering of our loves. When a person has his loves in the right order, we call him *pure of heart*.

That phrase, *pure of heart*, makes many of us a little uncomfortable. It implies that being pure of body won't cut it. It's not enough to do good and avoid evil: we have to love good and hate evil. But why does God care what we love or hate, as long as we do the right thing? Besides, how can we change our tastes? (And even if we *could* change our tastes, doesn't that sound a bit like self-brainwashing?)

The first question is easy to answer. "Blessed are the pure of heart," says the Master, "for they shall see God." Only those who love goodness will seek the good; only those who love God will seek God; and those who seek will find. It's just that easy.

Then again, it's really not that easy after all. Men are hardwired to be promiscuous; it's unnatural for us to be satisfied with just one woman. And yet Christ not only commands us to be monogamous; He forbids us even from looking at another woman with lust. Likewise, though it's natural for us to love our brethren — our friends — according to Jesus, that's not enough. After all, "Do not even the tax collectors do so?" Rather, He says, "you shall be perfect, just as your Father in heaven is perfect." And that means loving everyone, each and every human being on the face of the earth, with an endless love. (Even for those who point out that *loving* is not necessarily the same as *liking* — which we are not commanded to do — it is a daunting task.)

The great glory of Christendom was that it helped us to order our loves properly. And it did so not only (or even principally) by outlawing vices such as prostitution, sodomy, and usury. It didn't merely take away the "near occasion of sin," as Catholics would call it. It nourished a Christian culture that taught humanity to seek the Good, affirm the True, and desire the Beautiful.

Another word for the *ordo amoris*, perhaps, is *imagination*, which comes from two Latin phrases. One is *imaginari*, meaning "to form an image." The other is *imaginatio*, meaning "fancy." It's not only our desire but the object of our desire and the lines we trace between the two. It's both our compass and our North. It's Dante's vision of Beatrice but also his love, his longing, and all his art.

Culture always has a role in forming our imagination, in ordering our loves, for better or worse. In the Age of Christendom, it was for the better. Today, not so much.

Ours is the disenchanted imagination, the pornographic imagination, the sadistic imagination, the capitalist imagination, the statist imagination, the satanic imagination. That's why the word *fantasy* has become a double entendre. It might mean something whimsical—but it might well be something vulgar, craven, or cruel.

Of course, to some extent, we are all disenchanted. None of us are immune to the Fall. We all suffer from *concupiscence*: a disordered love of sin. But part of us also and always wants to reclaim the innocence of Eden. It's this desire—the desire for simple, childlike goodness—that our culture tries to throttle in its crib.

Here, I think, we come to an important distinction. Many conservatives seem to feel that premodern man was entitled to innocence, just as he was entitled to enchantment—but that we are no longer so blessed. That, however, is wrong. We've always had to fight for one as much as the other. True, society used to be on our side and is no longer. Yet there has never been an age when Christians' hearts and minds were not assailed by demonic temptations and delusions of one kind or another.

So, how do we properly order our loves? How do we reform our imagination? The answer is: carefully.

The first step is the most important and yet (at least in Western Christendom) the most often neglected. We have to discipline our minds by quieting the *logismoi*: the constant deluge of thoughts, feelings, desires, appetites, passions, and anxieties that flood our minds. This is crucial, first of all, for achieving inner peace and prayer of the heart. For our purposes, however, it's also crucial for mastering the imagination.

The Fathers of the Church warn us that the imagination is the part of the mind most susceptible to demonic attack. We can resist breaking our Lenten fast if we don't imagine all the delicious foods we could be eating right now. We can resist watching pornography until we start actively fantasizing about sex. We can resist the temptation to despair until we start imagining the Boschian horrors that await us in Hell.

The Desert Fathers developed a method called *hesychasm* for mastering the mind and overcoming the logismoi. *Hesychasm* comes from the Greek *hēsychia* and simply means "stillness" or "quietude" in Greek. This is the aim of hesychastic prayer: to create a state of inner peace and silence in which the still, small voice of God can be heard. The most common and effective form of hesychasm is the practice of the Jesus Prayer, which we discussed in chapter 5.

Now's not the time to go into much detail. Let's just say, the matter is not as simple as replacing a "bad imagination" with a "good imagination." Imaginations are good and useful things. They are gifts from God. Indeed, it's by using the imagination that we come nearest to understanding the power of our Creator God. But just as the most glorious angels became the most wretched demons, so too the imagination becomes the source of both ineffable beauty and unspeakable ugliness. As Saint Hesychios the Priest warns us, "Only by means of a mental image can Satan fabricate an evil thought and insinuate this into the intellect in order to lead it astray."

Now, let's assume we've mastered the imagination—or at least begun to try. We've broken the mind like a wild bronco. How do we make it work for us? How do we transform it into a *good* imagination—one that is worthy of its freedom, of our trust?

Hooper's story about Lewis is a nice springboard. On the face of it, nothing seems more pragmatic than reading a newspaper; nothing could be less practical than reading a three-volume novel about hobbits and elves. Yet as a journalist, I can't help but point out that no journalist has ever been canonized. Few have felt themselves being drawn closer to God by reading the opinion page.[11] Yet, as I mentioned, countless souls have been converted by reading fantasy novels, not least of all C. S. Lewis. Our friend recalls reading George MacDonald's *Phantases* as a sixteen-year-old atheist:

> It is as if I were carried sleeping across the frontier, or as if I had died in the old country and could never remember how I came alive in the new.... Up till now each visitation of Joy had left the common world momentarily a desert, "The first touch of the earth went nigh to kill." Even when real clouds or trees had been the material of the vision, they had been so only by reminding me of another world; and I did not like the return to ours. But now I saw the bright shadow coming out of the book into the real world and resting there, transforming all common things and yet itself unchanged. Or, more accurately, I saw the common things drawn into the bright shadow. *Unde hoc mihi?* In the depth of my disgraces, in the then invincible ignorance

---

[11] The cult of G. K. Chesterton, however, is a notable one that shows how God indeed works in mysterious ways.

of my intellect, all this was given me without asking, even without consent. That night my imagination was, in a certain sense, baptized; the rest of me, not unnaturally, took longer. I had not the faintest notion what I had let myself in for by buying *Phantastes*.

I'd wager that most Christians can remember the moment their imagination was "baptized," the moment when they fell in love with Truth and Goodness and Beauty. For Malcolm Muggeridge, it was meeting Mother Teresa. For Rod Dreher, it was stepping into Chartres Cathedral. Sometimes these are conversion experiences. Usually, the actual conversion comes later. But when we do finally meet the Lord, we will think back to that day and say, "I remember when you first spoke to me."

Even so, it takes a fair bit of time and effort to keep up a well-formed imagination. We can't keep our hearts trained on the Good, the True, and the Beautiful if we feed them vulgar, false, and ugly things. We have to be discriminating. We must transform our homes, our communities, our very selves, into little bastions of Christian civilization. We have to take *personal responsibility* for keeping the flame of Christendom alive in our own hearts and for "sending fire on the earth."

But we must take particular care in knowing what to avoid. If you eat Taco Bell for supper every night, you're going to get sick. It doesn't matter if you eat salads for lunch. Poison is poison.

I think it's quite poignant that Lewis identified newspapers as one of those things that leaves us spotted by the world. "News" itself seems so neutral. But it's not, really. News media—whether it's slick corporate fare, or a home-cooked blog—invariably stamps us with a worldly phronema. Whether we're reading about the presidential primary or celebrity gossip, it makes no difference. *By its nature*, the news can deal only with the City of Man. It trains us to care about things that ultimately don't matter. As Saint Augustine asked, "What does it matter under whose government a dying man lives?"

A few years ago, I visited a monastery and was surprised to find that the monks had a subscription to both the *Boston Herald* and the *Boston Globe*. When I asked the prior about it, he smiled and said, "That's how we know who to pray for." I suppose that's one good reason to read the papers. But what else can they do for us? What can they tell us, except what we already know: that the world is full of sin and suffering and death?

It's the same with digital technology. We assume that smartphones and social media are neutral, that we get out what we put in. But this, too, is a lie—and one that becomes more evident with each passing day.

In one sense, technology seems like the opposite of "the news." It divorces us from reality. It transforms us into *devices* like itself: amalgams of light and sound and stimuli, determined by the algorithms we're fed by the programs we consume. Back in 2015, scientists found that the average American had an attention span of 8.25 seconds, less than that of a goldfish. Imagine how much that number has fallen today.

This takes disenchantment to a new level. We're no longer imprisoned in a materialist world; now we're trapped in little black boxes. Materialism looks like a palace compared with where we are now. We're like Squidgicum-Squees that swallow themselves.

When Christians complain about modern technology, they're almost always talking about Internet porn. And that's a big problem, bigger than we can imagine. And yet it's still only a symptom of a much larger malaise. Modern man is being subsumed, abolished, by a digital oblivion of our own making. We're uncreating ourselves.

Really, when you think about it, Internet porn and Internet news have a great deal in common. Both are highly addictive. That's how they're designed. Porn's hook is pleasure; the news feeds us fear. We're taught to believe that we can take control of our appetites and even determine the way history unfolds. And yet, the more we watch, the lonelier we get; and the more we read, the more powerless we feel.

These artifacts of modernity also make it virtually impossible to live a Christian life. You cannot be a mystic if you own a smartphone. Let me repeat that: *you cannot be a mystic if you own a smartphone.* These machines are designed to make your mind and your heart restless. And our hearts are always restless until they rest in the Lord.

Our little black rectangles are the essence of the "spot" that sin leaves on our souls. My friend Michael Dominic Taylor, a brilliant young Catholic philosopher, calls them palantírs, portals through which the evils of the world flow into our homes and into our souls. We feed them our fears, ambitions, and desires; and a torrent of corruption and lies pours forth in a ceaseless, demonic whisper. The sensible thing to do would be to banish them from our lives.

Study after study also shows that the more we use "smart" technology, the angrier we become. Studies have shown that online debates activate the same pleasure centers of our brain as road rage. We become addicted to our own malice. This technology is a threat to Christian charity.

Simply put, both porn and the news train us to obsess over what Saint John the Beloved calls "all that is in the world": "the lust of the flesh, and the lust of the eyes, and the pride of life."

What do you think is the most ageless theme in all of literature? Probably war. From the *Iliad* to the *Aeneid* to *Beowulf* to the *Song of Roland* to *Gawain and the Green Knight* to the *Poem of the Cid*, nothing so powerfully captures man's imagination.

Thanks to modern windbags like Flaubert and Joyce, we tend to think of art as something delicate and brooding. But before the modern era, art was *exciting*. This is why, in decadent societies like ours, only great warriors—like Tolkien and Lewis, who were soldiers in WWI and soldiers of the cross—can produce great art. The great dreamers are always great doers.

Speaking of war, is it a coincidence that our entertainment has become more and more violent as fewer and fewer of our citizens serve in the armed forces—and even our conflicts are fought by snipers and drones? This is merely another kind of uncreation and disenchantment. We're amused by the idea of taking another person's life because we literally have no idea what that means. In ancient Rome, blood sports were popular in the final years before the Empire succumbed to its decadence. Alienation and sadism always go hand in hand.

And what is the flip side of blood sports? Vegetarianism and veganism. These fads have emerged only in the last century or so. It is no coincidence that in this same period farmers and herdsmen went from twenty-five percent of the American population to 1 percent. It's a proven fact that folks who raise and slaughter their own animals are far less likely to have moral qualms about eating meat. Such qualms are unique to modern Westerners, folks who buy their food, packaged in plastic, from grocery stores.

Of course, some ancient civilizations shunned meat-eating on theological grounds. India springs to mind, as does Japan. In fact, in many religious traditions, there's an understanding that men and women who attain high levels of spiritual mastery will adopt a plant-based diet. For example, Orthodox monks and Catholic contemplatives (Carthusians, Trappists, and so forth) usually forgo meat.

Partially, of course, this is about fasting. But it also has to do with compassion for animals. As Saint Isaac the Syrian wrote,

> A man with such a heart as this thinks of the creatures and looks at them, his eyes are filled with tears because of the overwhelming compassion that presses upon his heart. The heart of such a man grows tender and he cannot endure to hear of or look upon any injury, even the smallest suffering, inflicted upon anything in creation. Therefore he never ceases to pray with tears even for the dumb animals.

So I'm not opposed to vegetarianism. Not by any means. I hope to die a herbivore. I just can't believe that throngs of Westerners are now achieving in their mid-twenties a level of loving-kindness toward the "dumb animals" that once took saints a lifetime of spiritual discipline to cultivate.

Put it this way: fasting and anorexia are not the same thing just because they both involve not eating. Those who practice fasting will conquer their appetite; those who suffer from anorexia are simply ruled by food in a different way. Likewise, the old Christian vegetarians were inspired to give up meat through a deep, hard-won sense of communion with all of creation. The new "secular" vegetarian comes across as squeamish and as repelled by creation itself.

This is the paradox about purity of heart. In order to remain "unspotted from the world," we have to remain closely in touch with it, particularly the natural world. Yes, it's important to read good books. But it's even more important to "touch grass," as the kids say.

Relish reality! And rid yourself of your iPhone. Get a Light Phone, a Wise Phone, or even a flip phone. Delete your social media accounts—all of them. Seek out spaces—wide-open ones. Work with your hands. Learn an instrument. Write poetry. Keep a journal. Paint. Draw. Garden. Whittle. Sew. Hunt. Hike. Camp. Sail. Fish. Take up birding. Go stargazing. Lift weights. Join a boxing gym.

Live! Live the kind of life that would inspire a poet or a songwriter. Fill your days with love, adventure, and struggle. Let your victories be glorious and your defeats tragic. Everyone and everything is a theophany: an eruption of God into His own creation. Each of them is a gift. Let's try to show some gratitude.

Our duty as Christians is to surround ourselves with true and good and beautiful things. We have to purge everything fake and evil and vulgar from our lives. This may sound like an indulgence, but that's only the worldly phronema talking. It's not an indulgence: it's a solemn Christian duty.

"Finally," as Saint Paul told the Philippians, "whatever is true, whatever is noble, whatever is right, whatever is pure, whatever is lovely, whatever is admirable—if anything is excellent or praiseworthy—think about such things."

10

The Guerilla Gospel

See how far away I have fled,
I have dwelt in the wilderness.

—Psalm 54:7

We are normal.
It is the irreligious who are freaks.

—Evelyn Waugh

The phrase "intentional community" gets a bad rap these days. It smacks of retreatism: the cardinal sin of modern conservatism. More than that, it seems selfish. Sure, it would be nice if we could band together with some like-minded families, buy a little compound somewhere in Vermont, homeschool our kids together, and live off whatever vegetables will can grow in the rocky soil; but this isn't Hobbiton! Don't you know it's only a matter of time until the "illiberal Left" takes control of the State and uses its power to crush its enemies? We have to stay and fight!

There are at least two things wrong with this narrative.

First, the critics of intentional community never explain what they mean by "fight." They're not talking about forming militias (thank God). They don't mean proselytize, either: these are the same folks who laugh at the idea of street evangelism. Some are involved in high-level politics and political journalism—which is admirable. But they can't explain what "fighting" looks like for the 99.999 percent of their comrades who don't belong to the influencer class.

There's voting, of course. And that's important. We might even do a bit of door-knocking, if we have an especially strong candidate. But this would take only a few hours every year. How do our influencer friends want us to spend the rest of our time? And why can't we knock on doors *while* building an intentional community?

I've yet to get a straight answer—but as far as I can tell, it seems to involve retweeting the influencers' tweets, buying subscriptions to the influencers' magazines, and donating money to the influencers' nonprofits and campaigns. Maybe I'm just cynical, but it almost seems as if political influencers have a vested interest in promoting a worldly phronema.

Secondly, and more importantly, we have no hope of withstanding the onslaught of modernity unless we build strong communities—and in the twenty-first-century West, any Christian community must be, in some way, intentional.

Why do we need community? First and foremost, for our children. I don't need to tell you all the ways in which the secular elite are working to indoctrinate Western children in their grotesque ideology. They have complete control of the public education system, the adoption system, the medical system, the benefits system, and the child welfare system. They'll proudly use our taxpayer-funded institutions to seduce our sons and inseminate our daughters with their values and to punish, or imprison, parents who try to fight back.

We have no choice but to withdraw from these systems as much as possible. No responsible Christian parents should send their children to a public school. Even private schools, including most that call themselves Christian, are compromised. There are a handful of faithful schools in most states, though they tend to be small and badly funded.[12] Homeschooling, I think, is a safer bet.

But children also need friends. And they need friends who come from loving, faithful homes like their own. They need to be raised in an environment where Christianity is the "default,"

[12] There are exceptions. Saint Gregory the Great Academy in Pennsylvania and Saint Martin's Academy in Kansas are both outstanding.

where virtue is seen as *normal*, and where degeneracy is called by
its name.

This means that parents must be mindful of the families they
interact with socially. You can (and should) keep your sons safe
from porn for as long as you can. Don't let your children have
smartphones; and supervise their computer use closely. Use adult-
content filters such as Qustodio, which are effective and essential.
But remember: if Timmy's friends have smartphones or laptops,
it's certain that he'll be exposed to pornography.

A few years ago, I became part of an "intentional community"
in New Hampshire. One of the first things that struck me was that
boys and girls were able to be friends from early childhood through
college without ever becoming awkward around each other. I think
the lack of access to porn was a huge factor. They hadn't been
trained to see each other as mere sexual objects.

Even when they do start dating, messy breakups are rare because
premarital sex is rare. Couples don't form the deeper emotional
bonds that come only from sexual intimacy until they've gotten
married, or (for those who slip up) are at least planning to do so.
That may seem inconceivable these days. But it's true. Growing up
without porn provides a lifelong advantage for governing sexual
urges.

Men can appreciate what a handy skill that would be. Women
can appreciate the benefit of growing up with boys with a high
level of sexual self-discipline.

It's not all about sex, though. It really is amazing how deep the
roots of faith can run. Of the dozens of children I've known who
were raised in our community, only two have left the Church, and
one (thank God) has already come back. They are not sheltered;
there's really no point in trying to shelter children anywhere in
New England. The children in our community love their Christian

faith. They love their Christian friends, their Christian family, their Christian community. They know that Christianity makes more sense than any of its antagonists.

At some point, too, they realize that their fellow Christians are happier and healthier than their non-Christian neighbors. They don't want to throw away the gift they've been given. They want to share it with others.

Here's the thing, though. It's almost impossible to feel this kind of deep conviction without a strong community. Children need to see a Christian society, even if only in microcosm, to compare it with our larger post-Christian society.

But adults need community, too, and for many of the same reasons. We need friends we can relax with and who will also encourage us in virtue. If we're struggling with a certain sin or suffering from certain doubts or if we're having trouble with our marriage or our children, we need friends we can confide in. But we also need to experience the beauty of common life.

I am constantly amazed, truly amazed, at how happy and wholesome—and fun—a faithful community can be. It makes everything *real*. When the world seems out of control, or when arguments about Church and State seem hopelessly abstract, I think about our friends and family here, and I think, "This is what I'm fighting for."

Of course, this idea is not new; it's as old as the Church herself. It goes all the back to the upper room, where the Apostles waited together for the other Comforter before going into the world to teach all nations. In the Christian East, it has a name: *sobornost*.

The concept of sobornost was refined by a group of Orthodox intellectuals known as the Slavophiles in response to a movement among the Russian elite to liberalize and "Westernize" the nation. The Slavophiles believed it was essential to understand Christendom, and its constituent nations, not in terms of borders or ethnicity or political allegiances but as a *spiritual* unity. Our fundamental identity must be as Christians; our first loyalty must be to the Church. As the author Konstantin Aksakov explained in a letter to Tsar Alexander II,

> The Russian people do not wish to govern. They desire to preserve for themselves, not political but internal communal life.... Having thus left the kingdom of this world to the state they, as a Christian people, choose another path: the path to inner freedom and the spirit, the path to the kingdom of Christ. "The kingdom of God is within you."

Catherine de Hueck Doherty also compared sobornost to Pentecost:

> The secret of becoming a community is total involvement in the other. It is a total emptying of oneself so that each of us can say, "I live; now, not I, but Christ lives in me" Then the Christian community will come into existence. Then, like the Holy Spirit who formed it, it will be a fire burning in our midst. And from this fire, sparks will kindle the whole earth!

Now, dear reader, you might point out that the Apostles retreated into the upper room out of fear. You might suggest that, at the time, they seemed to have forgotten entirely about the Lord's promise to send His Spirit, the Spirit of Truth, to bide with them forever. They weren't practicing "intentional community" as much as they were hiding from the Jews. And you might be right. But the fact is that, *without* the Spirit, all their works would have been in vain.

They needed to go on retreat, whether they knew it or not. And so do we. The fewer our numbers, the slimmer our chances of victory—and the more we need sobornost.

This is why, even after Pentecost, the early churches[13] became a nation unto themselves. As Philip Sherrard observed,

> Originally Christianity possessed no legislation applicable to the social order, nothing which corresponds to the *shariyah* of Islam. It constituted a kind of society within a society, again like the pre-Christian mystery religions; and Christians had to survive in spite of society and its laws, not with their support and protection. In fact, they possessed if anything the idea that there was a clear and categorical line of demarcation between the realm of the state and that of the Church.

This is why the Church came to develop into a kind of mutual aid organization as well as a religious institution, as we discussed in chapter 8. For Christianity, political power is unnecessary. It's not a bad thing to have, by any means. But it's not an end in itself, or even a good in itself. God may want us to have such power, or He may not. It may have been good for us in the year 1024 but not in 2024. That's entirely up to Him.

Community, on the other hand, is integral to the Christian life. Except for the holiest of men and women—namely, hermits—it is absolutely essential to living out our Faith.

But if you prefer, think of intentional community as the mountain hideout in a guerilla war. The point of the hideout isn't actually to hide but to regroup. It's somewhere to train new recruits, clean our weapons, and tend to our wounds. But we still have bands of warriors going down into the villages and towns, engaging the Enemy and winning new converts to the Cause.

---

[13] That is, local churches (the Church in Rome, the Church in Corinth, the Church in Ephesus, and so on).

Really, what's the alternative? The critics of the Benedict Option and other communitarian movements seem to believe that we have a duty to be isolated and obscure. Some go even further and counsel us to put ourselves in the belly of the beast. Propaganda such as *God's Not Dead* will convince some parents to send their children to public schools and progressive colleges. They want their little boys and girls to be a "light unto the nations," winning over their fellow students and even their teachers and professors by a shining witness to the Faith. They will fail. They won't evangelize the institutions; they will be evangelized by the neo-pagans—and they will be destroyed.

Humans are like wolves. We're strong only in numbers. The "lone wolf" is sick or an aging alpha who has been expelled from the pack. He hunts alone, and so he dies alone.

There are communities, however, that are much superior to "intentional community"—namely, *unintentional* communities. When a group of Christians points to a map and decides to settle *there*, it almost never goes well. (Look at the tragedy of the Veritatis Splendor community in Texas.) The most successful experiments in sobornost happen somewhat by accident. They begin with an *anchor institution*: an exceptional parish, monastery, school, university, or business. Gradually, folks begin moving to the area in order to pray, study, or work. Faithful Christians begin to connect with one another through contact with these institutions. They develop friendships. They meet future spouses. They form new businesses. They start homeschool co-ops or found private schools. Within a few decades, the community has grown to a thousand or more.

These communities also win converts from the local population. It takes time. They haven't yet succeeded in reconverting the continental United States. But their success in retaining believers in an age of mass apostasy proves their efficacy.

And the howling lone-wolfers, despite being far more numerous, are faring much worse. They're not winning new converts; they're not even trying. While they're wrestling for control of the City of Man, they struggle to pass the Faith on even to their own children, never mind the "cafeteria Catholics" and Christmas-and-Easter Christians who are their neighbors. It's tragic, but true.

To be clear, I'm not saying that everyone has to pack up their lives and move to Front Royal, Virginia, or Moscow, Idaho. There are flourishing communities in many places: Dallas, Pittsburgh, Washington, and Nashville, to name just a few. My sources tell me they're blossoming in the environs of Boston and New York as well, which is cause for great hope. But wherever you are, and wherever you go, be sure to find the Rock on which you and your family can build a life of faith. Those who build on sand will be swept away.

11

People, Look East

In return for my loving them they kept on
accusing me falsely, but I kept on praying;
they repaid me evil for good and hatred for my love.

Psalm 108:4–5

The Church is in its infancy.

—Fr. Alexander Men

I've written a lot about mystics and missionaries, but before I close, I must now turn to *martyrdom*. The truth is, I've been avoiding the subject, because it's hard to know what to say. I'm not martyr; not yet, at least. And the thought of martyrdom is unnerving.

But I do believe the Western Church is about to enter a new Age of Martyrs. There's no doubt in my mind about that.

Still, most of the folks who warn about a coming wave of anti-Christian persecution fall into one of two categories: sensationalists, grifters, who prey on people's (legitimate!) fears for the sake of fame and fortune; or fragile snowflakes, in the Talebian sense. They're ready to canonize themselves for getting banned from Twitter—because that's *literally* the worst suffering they've ever had to endure.

I'd like to avoid both sensationalism and snowflakery. So let me spell out exactly what I mean by "persecution."

Within our lifetime, it will become truly dangerous to practice the Christian faith. In 2020, there were about three hundred attacks on Christian churches; this was only the beginning of a new trend. Vandalism, firebombing, and other acts of desecration will become commonplace. Services and liturgies will be disrupted. Parishioners will be assaulted. Some, no doubt, will be killed.

Christian couples will not be allowed to adopt or foster children. (This is already happening in some places.) Christian parents will lose custody of their children if they fail to affirm their children's sexuality or "gender identity." (This, too, is already happening in some places.) Governments will move to abolish or strictly control alternative forms of education, such as homeschooling, in order to ensure that every American student is indoctrinated in the same radical, secular ideology. Banks, insurance providers, and other companies will refuse to hire or service Christians, arguing that our faith conflicts with their "corporate values."[14]

Soon it will be legal to discriminate against Christians in the economic sphere. Those who refuse to identify as "allies" of the homosexualist movement, or to use the "preferred pronouns" of transgender colleagues, will be disciplined or fired with impunity. Pastors who preach traditional Christian morals will be charged under laws against hate speech, not conversion therapy. Many will go to prison. Churches and parishes that maintain orthodox standards will lose tax-exempt status, forcing many into bankruptcy. Many others will be forced to shut down under new, more aggressive laws meant to combat "religious extremism."

This, I think, is the best-case scenario. It is easy to imagine things getting much, much worse.

Many conservatives predict the return of militant, Soviet-style atheism, which is entirely possible. Yet, as we've already discussed, given the momentum toward re-enchantment, I think it's actually far more likely that Christendom will be replaced by a true, honest-to-goodness neo-paganism. Much like the old paganism, it

---

[14] As Rod Dreher points out in his book *Live Not by Lies*, such "soft totalitarian" methods are already being used across the Western world.

will applaud itself for its "tolerance" while it indulges in a bullying "intolerance."

This is what the fall of Christendom will look like for us here in the West. And it will be terrible. I'm afraid it will be more terrible than any of us can possibly imagine.

We should neither run toward nor away from martyrdom. To the best of our ability, we should refuse to allow persecution—or the fear of future persecution—to influence our judgment one way or the other. We should simply do the work that the Lord has set before us. We should love God and our neighbor. We should preach the Gospel to all nations. And we should steel ourselves with the example of those who came before us.

Remember when Saint Peter refused to accept that Our Lord had to die on the cross in order to fulfill His mission. What did the Master say?

> "Get behind me, Satan! You are an offense to me, for you are not mindful of the things of God, but the things of men." Then Jesus said to His disciples, "If anyone desires to come after me, let him deny himself, and take up his cross, and follow me. For whoever desires to save his life will lose it, but whoever loses his life for my sake will find it. For what profit is it to a man if he gains the whole world, and loses his own soul? Or what will a man give in exchange for his soul? For the Son of Man will come in the glory of His Father with his angels, and then he will reward each according to his works."

Think also of Saint Ignatius of Antioch, who wrote in his *Epistle to the Romans*, shortly before he was mauled to death in the amphitheater:

> I am writing to all the Churches and state emphatically to all that I die willingly for God, provided you do not

interfere. I beg you, do not show me unseasonable kindness. Suffer me to be the food of wild beasts, which are
the means of my making my way to God. God's wheat
I am, and by the teeth of wild beasts I am to be ground
that I may prove Christ's pure bread. Better still, coax
the wild beasts to become my tomb and to leave no part
of my person behind: once I have fallen asleep, I do not
wish to be a burden to anyone. Then only shall I be a
genuine disciple of Jesus Christ when the world will not
see even my body.

And of Saint Polycarp (+155), who, before being burned at the
stake, prayed to God:

I give you thanks that you count me worthy to be numbered
among your martyrs, sharing the cup of Christ and the
resurrection to eternal life, both of soul and body, through
the immortality of the Holy Spirit. May I be received this
day as an acceptable sacrifice, as you, the true God, have
predestined, revealed to me, and now fulfilled. I praise you
for all these things, I bless you and glorify you, along with
the everlasting Jesus Christ, your beloved Son.

Or the blessed Origen (+253), a later Father of the Church who
looked back to the age of persecution wistfully, almost nostalgically:

People were faithful then, when intense martyrdoms
were occurring. We used to come back to our gatherings
from the burial places after we had followed the martyrs
to their graves. The whole church would be gathered
without depression. The catechumens, neither frightened
nor troubled, were instructed by the martyrdoms and the
deaths of those confessing the truth unto death before the

living God. The faithful were few at that time, but they were genuinely faithful.

Of course, this was not the end of persecution but merely a lull therein. And yet when the bloodshed resumed, Christians remained resolute. So says Saint Cyprian (+258):

> Although this mortality has contributed nothing else, it has especially accomplished this for Christians and servants of God, that we have begun gladly to seek martyrdom while we are learning not to fear death. These are trying exercises for us, not deaths; they give to the mind the glory of fortitude: by contempt of death they prepare for the crown.

And we could go on—and on and on. Yet we needn't even look to ancient history. Remember that, for our brothers in the Eastern churches, Christendom fell a long, long time ago. For the Antiochian Church, it fell in the seventh century, when the Rashidun Caliphate took the Levant from Byzantium. For the Greek Church, it fell in 1453 with the walls of Constantinople. For the Russian Church, it fell in 1918 when Bolsheviks shot Tsar Nicholas II and his family.

Whether it has been a hundred years or thirteen centuries, these churches have existed in a "post-Christian" world. Their experiences aren't all the same. It's easier to be a Christian in Russia than in Turkey. Still, all Eastern Christians, both Orthodox and Catholic, have gone through what we're going through now. They know what it is like to have power; they know what it is like to lose it.

Eastern Christians know that the Church can and will survive the fall of Christendom. And not only can she withstand persecution; she can flourish in its very midst.

AFTER CHRISTENDOM

Today, the three most religious nations in Europe—Romania, Cyprus, and Greece—are Orthodox. All three were subject to the genocidal Ottoman Empire for centuries. Romania also suffered under Nicolae Ceaușescu, one of the most vicious (though inept) dictators in history.

Meanwhile, the Russians lived just recently under a regime of brutal state atheism for the better part of a century. Father Mikel Hill observes that "by even conservative reports, more than 12 million Orthodox Christians were killed for their faith under the Soviets; in 1937 alone, 85,300 Orthodox clergy were shot." Imagine if China conquered the United States and, simply to make a point, eradicated the whole population of Los Angeles. That's about 12 million souls.

The Church in Russia today is descended from those men and women who persevered in the faith through a century of vicious persecution. And the axiom proved true: the blood of the martyrs is indeed the seed of the Church. As Metropolitan Kallistos observed,

> What effect did Communist propaganda and persecution have upon the Church? In many places there was an amazing quickening of the spiritual life. Cleansed of worldly elements, freed from the burden of insincere members who had merely conformed outwardly for social reasons, purified as by fire, the true Orthodox believers gathered themselves together and resisted with heroism and humility.

In the last thirty years, Russian Orthodoxy has seen exponential growth. According to Pew, "Between 1991 and 2008, the share of Russian adults identifying as Orthodox Christian rose from 31 percent to 72 percent." The Russian Orthodox church has also built roughly thirty thousand churches in the last ten years.

Orthodoxy remains a strong presence in other parts of the former Soviet Union, such as Ukraine.

Meanwhile, religious faith in the rest of the Western world has been declining sharply. Our apostasy isn't the result of persecution. It's entirely voluntary. We have allowed ourselves to be seduced away from the Church. And our own institutional churches have given us very little reason to stay.

What makes the Orthodox churches so resilient? I think there are a few key factors.

I. Inculturation

Wherever they traveled, and whenever they encountered a new people, Orthodox missionaries took care to translate liturgical texts into the vernacular. This is most obvious in the case of Cyril and Methodius, the Apostles to the Slavs. When these great saints realized that the Slavs had no written language, they simply invented one. Today, all Slavic languages are descended from their "Old Church Slavonic." They also use the basic alphabet them the missionaries gave them, aptly named "Cyrillic."

There are a few glaring exceptions to this rule, most notably the Church of Antioch. Until the seventeenth century, the Patriarch of Antioch was effectively appointed by the Patriarch of Constantinople, and the latter almost always chose a fellow Greek. The liturgy was also conducted solely in Greek. But as Archbishop Anastasios of Albania points out in his book *Mission in Christ's Way*, this was because, before the advent of Islam, most Christians in the Near-East had been ethnic Greeks and Jews. When the Arab people were dispersed across the region through the Islamic conquests of the seventh century, they became an ethnic majority—and indeed, the majority of Christians were Arab as well. But old habits die hard, and by then, the liturgical language had calcified.

The "failure to inculturate" meant that Arabs struggled to feel a true sense of belonging in the Church of Antioch, even though thousands of them were martyred every year by the Muslim authorities. Many simply felt that Christianity was a Greek religion, not an Arab one. By contrast, Islam is a quintessentially Arabic faith; technically, Muslims aren't even supposed to translate the Qur'an. For those not endowed with deep religious convictions, the choice wasn't terribly hard.

II. Beauty

Eastern Christians have always placed a high premium on beautiful church architecture. As Archbishop Anastasios explains, Orthodox Christians see "the temple's beauty as a visible symbol of God's glory in space."

Interestingly, as so many Roman Catholics and Protestants have embraced modernist architecture, Eastern Catholics and Orthodox have taken great pains to preserve their traditional style of church-building. This seems particularly surprising, given that these parishes tend to be smaller and poorer.

Then again, maybe it's not surprising at all. Congregations and denominations that embrace contemporary (read: *ugly*) architecture generally do so for ideological rather than economic reasons. They wish to appear more accessible, less elitist. Even if the goal is admirable, the method typically fails.

In any case, this simply isn't a concern for most Eastern Christians living in the West. They don't come from the same cultural context. Outside the "developed world," almost no one would ever think to build an ugly building *on purpose*. The one exception, of course, was the former Soviet Union. Yet, even there, ugly modernist architecture was identified explicitly with the communist oppressors; beauty was the hallmark of the ancient Christian heritage.

To be clear, not all modern Eastern churches are beautiful, nor are all Western churches ugly. Eastern Christians have no monopoly on beauty. But beauty has remained a central and uncontroversial ideal for Eastern Christians in a way that it hasn't for Roman Catholics or Protestants—and beauty has been critically important to their survival, and even flourishing, in the face of persecution.

III. Simplicity

In eighth-century Byzantium, the faithfully orthodox *iconodules* defended the use of icons, which they revered as beneficial for worship. Nevertheless, they distinguished themselves by their simple manner of dress, for which they were mocked by the heretical *iconoclasts*, who opposed the use of icons.

In the West, this seems inconsistent. When we think of ornate churches, we think of elaborate vestments. By contract, it is the Puritans, in their drab black cloaks, who seem at home in sparsely appointed meetinghouses.

Why is this? At some point, we began to set beauty and simplicity at odds. That is why reformist movements, from Puritanism to the Second Vatican Council, have tended to prefer plainer, less formal styles of worship. It is why (again) some go even further down that path, to the point of intentionally making their churches and liturgies ugly. They see it as a way of living the Gospel's call to poverty: a voluntary self-emptying, both physical and spiritual, for the sake of God and neighbor.

But in the Eastern Church, beauty is always joined with simplicity. Iconography *by its nature* is simple. It rejects the intricacy and realism of both pagan and Western religious art. Nevertheless, it is profoundly beautiful. Likewise, the architecture of Hagia Sophia is gorgeous; but it is rather uncomplicated compared with the infinitely complex (though no less beautiful) cathedrals of Western Europe. Think of Chartres, for example, or Canterbury, and you will appreciate the difference.

While Eastern vestments can, of course, be quite striking—especially the splendid jewel-encrusted miters worn by some bishops—these are reserved exclusively for religious functions; when the priest is serving at the altar, he is a sort of living icon of Christ the High Priest. But the Eastern clergyman's "everyday" clothing is always the same, whether he's a parish priest or a patriarch: a simple black cassock, perhaps with a pectoral cross and a plain black miter. Outside the context of the liturgy, these clergymen are all simply servants of God. Even the scholar Frithjof Schuon, an apostate from Roman Catholicism to Sufi Islam, realized as much:

> It is very unlikely that Christ, who washed the feet of his disciples and who taught them that the first shall be last, would have appreciated the imperial pomp of the Vatican court: such as the kissing of the foot, the triple crown, the *flabelli*, the *sedia gestatoria*; to the contrary, there is no reason to think that he would have disapproved of the ceremonies—of sacred total and not imperial style—which surround the orthodox patriarch.

In this way, Eastern Christians are able to "worship the Lord in the beauty of holiness" without compromising either beauty *or* holiness.

IV. Mysticism

The Jesus Prayer is a form of meditation developed by the Desert Fathers and refined by Saint John Cassian in the fourth century. To this day, it remains central to Eastern spirituality for laymen, clergy, and monastics alike.

The simplicity and uniformity of Orthodox spirituality is critical. Roman Catholics value a variety of "vocations," including lay, religious, and secular. There are many different spiritualities, as represented by various Third Orders. There's a plethora of private devotions, from variations of the Rosary to chaplets to novenas to scapulars and many more. In addition, there are numerous supplementary practices of worship, from daily Mass to Eucharistic Adoration to the Stations of the Cross.

In the East, there is one, well-trodden path toward the Truth, which is Jesus Christ. It might be said that, aside from the Divine Liturgy, this path has three pillars: chanting the Psalter, studying the Scriptures, and praying the Jesus Prayer. These three pillars are basically the same for every Eastern Christian, regardless of his station in life. While the monk may have more time to devote to the Jesus Prayer than a married man, the difference is only one of degree, not of kind.

In other words, for the Orthodox, there is really only one way of being Christian. All the faithful are called to embrace one form of "spirituality," which has a single purpose: to foster a deep, intimate, and personal relationship between the soul and God using the fundamental tools given to us by the Patriarchs, Prophets, Apostles, and Fathers.[15]

In times of plenty, a large repertoire of spiritual approaches may benefit the Church. But in times of persecution, the intimacy of a shared experience may be required to sustain her.

---

[15] The most "modern" of these devotions, the Jesus Prayer, is usually dated to the 400s, but Saint John Chrysostom claims it was handed down to us by Saint Paul!

V. Asceticism

If you know anything about Eastern Christianity, you probably know about Great Lent. Traditionally, Orthodox and Byzantine Catholics will abstain from all meat, dairy, oil, and wine during the forty days leading up to Easter. As it happens, three major fasts of this sort are also observed throughout the year. There is also the Apostles' Fast, the Nativity Fast, and the Dormition Fast.

Today, this focused regimen often sounds extreme even to the most devout Roman Catholics. Yet it used to be commonplace in the West as well. Now, the question is this: Did persecution sustain the Eastern Church? Or did persecution itself strengthen the East in its discipline, while the softness and ease of life in the West made us too weak to persist?

VI. Mission

Just as Western Catholics largely came to view mysticism as a particular "vocation" reserved for contemplative monks and those blessed with extraordinary supernatural graces (such as visions), the Roman Church also developed a class of professional missionaries: the friars. As a rule, laymen were disengaged from the duties of evangelism.

Some Protestant groups tried to buck this trend. Quakers and Methodists, for instance, were well known for their zealous lay missionaries. Even the Swedenborgians and Universalists had their share of soapbox preachers. But that zeal tended to fade over time. Eventually, most denominations developed *missionary societies*, funded by the laity. As in the Catholic Church, this led to the "professionalization" of evangelism.

In the late twentieth century, both Protestants and Catholics reinvigorated their professional evangelical efforts. Evangelical

Protestantism spread widely and was matched by the Catholic Church's "New Evangelization." Indeed, both enjoyed some measure of success thanks to televangelists such as Billy Graham and Fulton Sheen. But neither has had much success in stemming the increasingly rapid tide of apostasy.

Meanwhile, the Eastern Church has preserved the vision of the Church Fathers. According to Archbishop Athanasios,

> Missionary activity was never the work of so-called "missionary experts"; people from every social class and group contributed. Monks and clergy carried the main weight of the task, but many laymen, laywomen, politicians, military men, and even prisoners contributed spontaneously to spreading the Gospel.

VII. Kerygma

What happens during the Lord's Supper? A Roman Catholic would say *transubstantiation*: the bread and wine is substantially transformed into the Body and Blood of Christ, leaving only the appearance of bread and wine. A Lutheran would probably say *consubstantiation*: the Body and Blood coexist with the bread and wine. An Anabaptist would almost certainly favor the Protestant view of *memorialism*: the belief that Holy Communion is not a sacrament at all but, rather, a symbolic re-creation of the Last Supper.

But if you're an Eastern Christian, you'll respond by quoting Matthew 26. The bread is Christ's Body; the wine is His Blood, which He shed for many for the remission of sins.

An Orthodox would certainly admit that his understanding of the Eucharist is much closer to the Catholic than the Lutheran, and to the Lutheran than the Anabaptist. But he'll generally decline to use the term *transubstantiation*. Why? Because the Lord's words are hard enough to understand. In John 6, Jesus says, "My flesh is meat indeed, and my blood is drink indeed." Many of His disciples thought to themselves, "This is an hard saying; who can hear it?" and abandoned Him (vv. 55, 60, 66). Yet He chose not to clarify Himself one way or the other. The Master chose to leave it at that.

This is one of the defining features of Eastern theology: a refusal to dogmatize. Orthodox simply have fewer doctrines than Catholics or Protestants. Many of the debates that divided the Christian West, the Orthodox simply were not party to. "Our religion is a matter of realities," Gregory Palamas said, "not of words." Eastern Christians don't try to explain the Mysteries of our Faith. They *embrace* the mystery. They allow themselves to be awed and humbled. According to Evagrius, "A theologian is one who prays, and one who prays is a theologian."

In the last few years, you may have heard trendy Christians talking about *kerygma*. It's a Greek word meaning "to proclaim" or "to herald." It refers to the kind of preaching used in the New Testament by Christ and His Apostles. It's not a rational argument. It doesn't appeal to the intellect, at least not at first. Rather, it confronts the hearer with simple, beautiful truths that address themselves directly to the heart. "Repent ye: for the kingdom of heaven is at hand." "Love one another, as I have loved you." "God hath made the same Jesus, whom ye have crucified, both Lord and Christ."

Because Eastern Christians take a minimalist view of dogma, theirs is a kerygmatic faith. It's not weighed down by human definitions. Eastern Christians don't divide themselves into rival schools and sects. They don't rely on their own intelligence or charm in leading souls into the Church. They let Christ speak for Himself. They allow the holy and life-giving mysteries to operate on the human heart.

It may be that dogmas and schools have their place. Among certain types of Christians, these arguments may do some good. Certain cultures (e.g., ancient Rome) are more regimented than others and have an ear tuned to formalistic argumentation.

But when you're confronting a world that doesn't know the Church—and maybe even *hates* the Church—subtle arguments won't do a lick of good. Our neighbors don't need to be persuaded. They need Jesus Christ. It is not in our power to bring them to Christianity: only Jesus can do that.

VIII. Primacy of Prayer

Let me say that again: *we cannot convert anyone.* Conversion is a matter of desire, and we can't convince (much less force) anyone to desire God. Only God, the Lover of mankind, can stir that desire in a person. Belief itself is a gift, and only God can give it. As George Herbert put it so beautifully:

> My God, what is a heart?
> That thou shouldst it so eye, and woo,
> Pouring upon it all thy art,
> As if that thou hadst nothing else to do?

This is why the mystics, from King Solomon to Augustine to John of the Cross, use erotic language to describe the inner life. God must seduce the sinner, using all His beauty, all His charm. He must tear down the walls of selfishness and sin that stand between Him and our souls—your soul; my soul—which He would ravish passionately for all eternity. This is His one desire, for which He would give His life. And did.

We can't do any of God's wooing for Him. But He *does* allow us to act as a kind of accomplice—to arrange a secret meeting between Himself and His lover, the soul of our fellow sinner.

He may even, in His infinite goodness, allow us to make the first introduction. And so we become minor heroes in His great epic romance. He is the dashing young King; we are His gallant chevaliers.

A good knight doesn't charge into the field without his prince's command, though, and a good compatriot doesn't choose His friend's lover for him. All we can do is wait for the orders to come down—the subtle nod, the knowing glance.

Eastern Christians have learned to live in this state of active anticipation. The Greek Fathers call this a state *nepsis*, meaning "wakefulness." The opposite of the neptic man is the drunkard or one who is in a stupor—which is not a bad way to describe the five foolish virgins who "slumbered and slept" and so failed to see the Bridegroom approaching.

But how did the Greek Fathers stay wakeful? Remember the answer from Father Seraphim Rose: they "walk" in the fear of God, trembling lest they lose His grace, which by no means is given to everyone, but only to those who hold the true Faith, lead a life of Christian struggle, and treasure the grace of God which leads them heavenward."

Eastern Christianity is sometimes charged by some Western Christians with quietism, or "monkishness." Yet Eastern Christians gladly own this critique. Saint Charbel Makhlouf makes this point beautifully. "Be monks in the world, even if you don't wear a habit," he says. "Fill the earth with prayer and incense."

Because the East refuses to make a distinction between different "vocations," every Christian is called to imitate Christ's perfect *kenosis*, or self-emptying. We are to abandon our own will and place ourselves in total obedience to the Father. In this way, the great pitfall of the modern world—what Father Alexander Schmemann called "activism"—is avoided.

Really, activism is the main antagonist of this book. According to Father Schmemann, the activist is a kind of Pelagian: "We are constantly called to repent for having spent too much time in contemplation and adoration, in silence and liturgy, for having not dealt sufficiently with the social, political, economic, racial, and all the other issues of real life."

Fr. Seraphim Rose went even further. He warned that the spirit of activism—the *desire* to remake the world, even according to a Christian ideal—plays right into the Enemy's hands:

> This is of course a very easy subject to get carried away with; but our Lord has told us to be prepared for the signs of the end, and those who are not interested in them are only going to be seduced by them. The faithful remnant of Christians in the last days, as our Lord has told us, will be very small; the vast majority of those who call themselves Christians will welcome Antichrist as the Messiah. Therefore it is not enough to be a "non-denominational" Christian; those who are not true Orthodox Christians belong to the "new Christianity," the "Christianity" of Antichrist. The Pope of Rome and practically everyone else today speaks of "transforming the world" by Christianity: priests and nuns take part in demonstrations for "racial equality" and similar causes. These have nothing to do with Christianity: they do nothing but distract men from their true goal, which is the Kingdom of Heaven. The coming age of "peace," "unity," and "brotherhood," if it comes, will be the reign of Antichrist: it will be Christian in name, but Satanic in spirit. Everyone today seeks happiness on earth, and they think this is "Christianity"; true Orthodox Christians know that the age of persecutions, which began again under the

Bolsheviks, is still with us, and that only by much sorrow and tribulation are we made fit to enter the Kingdom of Heaven.

If I could leave you with only one thought, it would be this: Western Christians are desperate to find some new system, some new strategy, that will save the West. My argument is not that, if we abandon ourselves to God's will—if we devote ourselves to prayer, fasting, almsgiving, and righteousness—we'll magically restore Christendom to its former glory. No: my argument is that we should devote ourselves to prayer, fasting, almsgiving, and righteousness because *that's what God wants us to do*. Our *desire* should be to please God.

If we're still hated, mocked, and persecuted—as I strongly suspect we will be—that doesn't mean our "strategy" has failed. It means that God, in His unfathomable wisdom and goodness, has chosen this lot for us. There is not—there never was—any guarantee of success, at least not in the world's terms.

Still, the experience of the Eastern Churches makes it clear that a post-Christian society is also a pre-Christian society. The ruins of Christendom have become a new mission field. Our is only to say, "Thy will be done."

Conclusion

The Greater Crusade

The mountain of God is sweet butter, a mountain of richly sweet butter. Why do you ponder other sweet mountains? This is the mountain where God dwells.

—Psalm 67:15–16

Completely have trust in God, leave everything in His hands, and believe that His love will act for your own benefit. Then God will take care of everything, because there is nothing He cannot do; everything is easy for Him. The difficult thing is for man to decide to humble himself and leave everything to God's providence and love.

—Saint Paisios of Mount Athos

In Islam, they speak of two jihads, or holy wars: the greater and the lesser. The lesser jihad is the one we in the West are familiar with. It's the violence, the collective struggle for dominance over all mankind, the subjugation of the whole world by and to the ummah. The greater jihad, however, is by man against himself. *Islam*, we know, means "submission," and a Muslim's first priority is to force himself to submit to Allah. Crucially, the lesser jihad can be waged only by those who complete the greater.

There is no equivalent to a lesser jihad in Christianity. The nearest we come is the Crusades, but they were not integral to the Faith. On the contrary, the spirit of the Crusades would have been alien to the Fathers, to the Apostles, and to Christ Himself.

In the First Book of Kingdoms, the Israelites are fighting (and losing) a war against the Philistines. They call upon God to "establish a king for us to judge us like all the other nations." God is displeased. Since the Lord led the Israelites out of Egypt, they had been ruled directly by God. Israel was a literal theocracy. "They have rejected me," God laments to the Prophet Samuel, "to bring to naught my reign over them." Samuel warns them that, in time, they will come to regret their decision: "Then in that day you will cry out before your king whom you chose for yourselves, and the Lord will not hear you in those days, because you chose a king for yourselves." Still, they cry: "Then we will be like all the other nations," they say, "and

our king will judge us and go out before us and fight our battles."
Samuel is distraught. "You have done great wickedness before the
Lord in asking a king for yourselves," he warns. Still, God grants
their request. He elects a man named Saul to serve as Israel's very
first king, and he quickly begins fighting Israel's battles for them.
Incidentally, the Philistines had destroyed every blacksmith in Israel;
the army had to confiscate every plowshare in the land and forge
them into armor and weapons.

Now, fastforward to the year A.D. 30. The Pharisees are waiting for God's anointed to restore the Kingdom of Israel, drive out
the Romans, and lead them to global domination. They know the
Scriptures so well, yet they can't see how deeply God abhors this
desire to rule and fight, to dominate and subjugate. They ask Jesus
when He, the alleged Messiah, plans to restore Israel. But Jesus
turns their question on its head. "The Kingdom of God is within
you," He tells them.

Christ has not come to restore the monarchy. He has come to
restore theocracy. Once again, God will rule His people directly.
This time, however, He will not reign over them. He will reign
within them. This is the Man of whom Isaiah spoke: the Word
of God, who shall judge all nations. At His coming, God's people
will beat their swords back into plowshares; "Nation shall not lift
up sword against nation, / Neither shall they learn war anymore."
The kingdoms of men know only tyranny and strife. The Kingdom
of God is freedom and peace.

And yet "the kingdom of heaven suffers violence," Jesus warns,
"and the violent take it by force." This violence is the war each of
us must wage against our passions, our appetites, our sins, our own
rebellious instincts, our satanic pride, to enthrone Christ within
our hearts. This is something very much like the greater jihad. It
is, so to speak, the greater crusade.

Christ also says, "Seek first the kingdom of God and His righteousness, and all these things shall be added to you." There is an impossible paradox at the bottom of our premise here. The only way Christians can ever rule the world is if we stop trying.

Now, here's the million-dollar question: Do you believe Jesus's promise? Do you trust Him to give you the whole world, if only you give Him yourself?[16]

And do we believe His promise that the meek shall inherit the earth? When you witness some grave injustice in the world—when the president signs an evil bill into law, or when innocent lives are lost in terrorist attack, or when a foreign leader slaughters his own people, or when one foreign country invades another—is your first response to become meeker?

Why do you think God said it was the meek who would inherit the world rather than the poor in spirit or the pure of heart? Because only the meek give God the opportunity to work through them. That's all "meekness" is. I think Metropolitan Anthony Bloom, of blessed memory, put it best:

> You remember how you were taught to write when you were small. Your mother put a pencil in your hand, took your hand in hers and began to move it. Since you did not know at all what she meant to do, you left your hand completely free in hers. This is what I mean by the power of God being manifest in weakness. You could think of that also in the terms of a sail. A sail can catch the wind and be used to maneuver a boat only because it is so frail. If instead of a sail you put a solid board, it would not work; it is the weakness of the sail that makes it sensitive to the wind. The same is

---

[16] Do *I*, for that matter?

true of the gauntlet and the surgical glove. How strong is the gauntlet, how frail is the glove, yet in intelligent hands it can work miracles because it is so frail.

We can't help God achieve His plan for salvation any more than a hammer helps the carpenter to build a house. The most we can do is allow Him to work with us, through us. And the more resigned we become to His will, the "weaker" we become, the more deeply and fundamentally we are united to Him. This is what it means to be the Body of Christ.

Of course, the acquisition of holy weakness (or meekness) is the work of a lifetime. It requires us to cultivate and maintain inner peace. And so much of what we consider "practical" is, in fact, totally counterproductive, if only because it robs us of this inner peace.

Again, without peace, a man can never be meek, and without meekness he cannot inherit the earth. That is why Saint Nikodemos urges us to guard our inner peace at all costs. "Watch yourself with all diligence," he writes, "lest the enemy rob you, depriving you of this great treasure, which is inner peace and stillness of soul. The enemy strives to destroy the peace of the soul, because he knows that when the soul is in turmoil it is more easily led to evil. You must guard your peace."[17]

This is where our journey together ends. There's nothing I as a journalist can do but point you beyond the world of journalism, current events, and politics (including, or especially, "Church politics"). Believe me, I've followed this road as far as it could take me, and it's a dead end. That world has nothing to offer you or anyone else.

Ultimately, the answers are not to be found in men like me or books like this. They're in Scripture and the Fathers. They're in

---

[17] For more on guarding our peace, see chapter 5. See also appendix A, on the Jesus Prayer.

the Divine Liturgy, or the Holy Mass, or whatever you prefer to call it. They're within you, dear reader. Remember what Saint Paul says: "You are an epistle of Christ" — yes, *you* — "written not with ink but by the Spirit of the living God, not on tablets of stone but on tablets of flesh, that is, of the heart."

Do you see how it always comes back to the heart?

You may have noticed that I haven't really addressed the question of *why* Christendom fell in the first place. I was hoping we could avoid that topic altogether, but I don't think that's possible. To put it briefly, I agree with Philip Sherrard: that, "if we live in a post Christian epic, this is not primarily because from somewhere toward the end of the seventeenth century we have deserted our Christian society. It may be because in creating and seeking to preserve the society we have sacrificed, or neglected, the essential character of Christianity itself."

This is the answer I've hinted at throughout the book, but let's state it now very clearly: God no longer reigns in the Western world because Western man drove Him from our hearts. We can't blame Islamists or Communists. Christendom committed suicide.

God is calling us to conversion. This is what the Master meant when He said, "Repent, for the Kingdom of God is at hand." He didn't mean, "Repent, because the Apocalypse is coming soon." He wasn't threatening us. He was telling us the Gospel, the *euangelion*, the Good News. The Jews wanted a worldly kingdom, free from the oppression of the Romans. But their Messiah offered something much greater: freedom from passion, the forgiveness of sins, and the friendship of God.

His message for us today is exactly the same: *The thing for which you long is close by you. It is imminent. It is within your very heart. All you have to do is repent. Give up your petty trinkets; they are worthless. I'll give you instead the Pearl of Great Price. Take off your rags and put on the wedding garment. Put not your trust in princes, for human salvation is emptiness. Instead, put your trust in me.*

We do not believe these promises because we are unconverted. We may call ourselves Christians, or go to church every Sunday, or wear a cross around our neck. None of it matters if we don't trust in Jesus's promises and live by His commandments. The Master warned us: "Not everyone who says to me, 'Lord, Lord,' shall enter the kingdom of heaven."

Please, dear reader, do not be offended. But let's not deceive ourselves in our pride either. Remember how certain Peter was in his own faith ... until he stepped outside the boat and began to sink. Remember how he insisted that he would never betray the Lord ... until he did, three times. Even at the very end of his life, he tried to escape martyrdom by fleeing Rome; only when Christ met him on the Appian Way, carrying His cross, did he turn back and face his own death.

Peter betrayed Christ no less than Judas did. The only difference between them was repentance. Peter was a sinner, but Judas was a hypocrite. We all sin, whether we want to or not; but we are hypocrites only by choice. And this is all I hoped to say in this book. Forget the "lesser crusade," the sin of the Pharisees. Embrace the greater crusade. Wage holy war against your own passions, your desires, your anxieties, and above all your doubts. The only Christendom that matters is within you. Don't pine for a king when God reigns within you. "Commune with your own heart," and there enthrone Christ. Repent, and believe the Good News: You *are* Christendom. Your heart is the only kingdom God desires. Go now and meet your King.

Come, O Lord.

Appendix A

A Guide to the Jesus Prayer

What is the Jesus Prayer?

There are several common forms of the Jesus Prayer. The two most popular are probably:

A. "Lord Jesus Christ, have mercy."

B. "Lord Jesus Christ, Son of God, have mercy on me, a sinner."

Form A is more traditional, because it's the more literal translation of the common Greek usage (*Kyrie Iesou Christe, eleison*). Form B is more popular in the English-speaking world because of the symmetry: there are two clauses in each "half" of the prayer, which makes it easier to incorporate rhythmic breathing. More on that in a moment.

Form B of the Jesus Prayer contains the four essential elements of prayer. It's an act of worship ("Lord Jesus Christ"), a confession of faith ("Son of God"), a plea for His beneficence ("have mercy on me"), and an act of penance ("a sinner").

At first, it might seem like penance ought to come before plea. But the funky order has deep significance. In the parable of the prodigal son, the father doesn't even wait for his prodigal son to apologize before rushing down the road to greet him with a kiss (Luke 15:20); likewise, God doesn't wait for us to repent before pouring out His goodness upon us. In fact, repentence is *itself* a fruit of His love. This is hugely important to Eastern theology. Confession doesn't restore us to a "state of grace"; confession is *evidence* of grace. God is always rushing down the road to greet us, His prodigal children, with a kiss.

The meaning of *mercy*

As I said, the word *mercy* in Greek is *eleison*. This comes from another Greek word, *eleos*, meaning "oil." Oil had many properties in the ancient world, and especially the Early Church, many of which might escape modern readers. Of course, oil was (and is) used to add flavor and texture to food. It is also used in rituals of anointing, such as the consecration of new bishops or the blessing of the sick. But it was also used as a salve for wounds and burns, a moisturizer, a hair product, and a perfume—both for the living and the dead.

This is what makes the Jesus Prayer so versatile. It is, in fact, as versatile as oil itself. When we ask God for His *eleison*, His mercy, we are not only asking Him to forgive our sins and heal our souls (though this is certainly the most important meaning of the prayer!). We are also asking for Him to pour out His goodness upon us. We are asking Him to bless us with every blessing.

Please note, I am not trying to soften or skirt the penitential nature of the Jesus Prayer. It must always be prayed in a spirit of repentance. My point is that the Jesus Prayer is not *only* a penitential prayer. The Jesus Prayer contains virtually every other prayer within itself. It is good for what ails you—and what don't.

The Jesus Prayer in the West

Some people believe that "Western Christians" (namely, Roman Catholics and Protestants) shouldn't pray the Jesus Prayer. At best, this stems from a fear that it won't fit into the general "rhythm" of their spiritual life. At worst, they simply turn up their noses at anything perceived as Eastern.

Yet it's worth remembering that the Prayer was refined in no small part by Saint John Cassian, a Western Father. True: over time, the Rosary came to occupy the same spiritual niche in the Western Church and sort of crowded out the Jesus Prayer. But the latter belongs as much to the Western tradition as the former.

Methods of praying the Jesus Prayer

Some people use the Jesus Prayer as an "arrow prayer": a short appeal to Heaven in times of suffering or trial. Let's say that someone cuts you off in traffic. You want to pull ahead of him, cut him off, and then brake-check him. Instead, you say, "Lord Jesus Christ, Son of God, have mercy on me, a sinner." God takes away your wrath, and you go on with your day. That's an arrow prayer.

And that's a great way to use the Jesus Prayer. In fact, it was developed by the Desert Fathers largely for that purpose: as a prayer that works for any occasion. It's like the Swiss Army knife of the spiritual life.

But it's also a form of meditation called "prayer of the heart." The goal is to repeat the Jesus Prayer so often, and so devoutly, that it becomes second nature, thus fulfilling Saint Paul's command to "pray without ceasing" (1 Thess. 5:17).

If we truly want to pray without ceasing—if we wish to make the Jesus Prayer a prayer of the heart—we must set aside time each day for its practice. Most folks use a prayer rope to count (traditionally, with one's left hand) the number of prayers they say in one sitting.

Others prefer to use a timer: they find this removes the temptation to rush through their prayers.

To be sure, it's better to say the Jesus Prayer with great compunction just once than to say it a thousand times with a wandering mind. Still, I prefer to use a prayer rope. Yes, my mind wanders. But when I use a timer, I find myself trying to guess how much time has passed, and when my phone is going to start barking at me. Plus, the tactile experience—counting knots—also helps to keep me grounded in the prayer. So to each his own.

The psychosomatic method

Most folks, when they pray the Jesus Prayer, will synch their prayers with their breathing, and vice versa. This is sometimes called the "psychosomatic method" because it incorporates both body and mind. This, too, is important to Eastern theology, which stresses the goodness of all creation, especially the human body. If you spend time in an Eastern church, you'll notice that, in both private and public worship, there's an effort to pray with the whole body, not just the head and the mouth.

The usual psychosomatic method is to pray "Lord Jesus Christ, Son of God" while breathing in and "Have mercy on me, a sinner" while breathing out.

If you listen to some of the most popular videos about the Jesus Prayer on YouTube, you might hear people—wise, holy people!—say that the psychosomatic method should be practiced only under the close direction of your spiritual father. They say it's dangerous to incorporate rhythmic breathing on your own. I've asked several priests about these potential "dangers." Not one of them had the faintest idea what I was talking about.

The one pitfall I can think of is this: much of what passes for psychosomatic prayer is really a kind of self-hypnosis. If you've ever witnessed Sufi meditation (dhikr circles, whirling dervishes, and so forth), it's easy to see where the "spiritual experiences" of its practitioners come from: hyperventilation with a side of vertigo. Such false ecstasies distract us from the true purpose of the Jesus Prayer, which is to unite ourselves to the Divine Trinity and enter into the divine nature.

Some recommend breaking the Jesus Prayer into four parts over two breaths, like this:

First, breathe in, "Lord Jesus Christ."
Second, breathe out, "Son of God."
Third, breathe in, "Have mercy on me."
Fourth, breathe out, "A sinner."

This (they say) allows us to slow down our breathing even further and dwell on each part of the prayer. I tried this method for about a year but ended up going back to the old one-breath method. In my opinion, the two breaths makes the prayer *too* slow—too rhythmic, too unlike natural speech. Also, by dwelling so long on each word, I feel as if I'm addressing myself instead of Christ. The Prayer becomes a mindfulness technique rather than a . . . well, a prayer.

Remember: you don't have to use the psychosomatic method at all. In fact, if you're brand-new to the prayer, it might be better *not* to.

Praying with the body

Eastern Christianity emphasizes the unity of body and soul. (This is present in Western Christianity too, of course, but not to the same extent.) That's why we commonly find practitioners of the Jesus Prayer incorporating some physical action. We engage the entire self. This allows us to glorify God more fully and to sanctify our whole person; it also keeps us focused and prevents us from becoming restless.

Some simply make the Sign of the Cross.

Others make a low bow at the waist.

Still others perform metanies—low bows in which one touches the ground with the back of one's right hand—followed by the Sign of the Cross.

Many saints, most famously Nektarios of Aegina, have made a full prostration:

A. Kneel down.

B. Place both fists on the ground, knuckles down, close to where your knees touch the floor.

C. Lower your head until it is nearly touching the ground.

If you do this right, you shouldn't simply be "on all fours," with your arms, legs, and back making straight lines. Rather, your body should be scrunched up into a ball. You shouldn't be resting comfortably. This is a posture of humility and submission; it should feel uncomfortable—and look a bit silly!

When to pray the Jesus Prayer

The ultimate goal is for the Jesus Prayer to become a "prayer of the heart," or self-activating prayer: one that we "say" within ourselves automatically, without even thinking about it. In the First Book of Kingdoms, Hannah describes God as "the One who gives a prayer to the one who is praying." When we become one with God, uniting ourselves entirely to Him, He pours out prayer within us endlessly. We cannot fulfill Saint Paul's command to "pray without ceasing," but God can.

Short of that, we should simply strive to pray the Jesus Prayer whenever we think of it.

Once again, it's essential that we set aside time every day to devote ourselves completely to the Jesus Prayer. The earlier, the better: as Lewis said, "No one in his senses would reserve his chief prayers for bedtime—obviously the worst possible hour for any action that needs concentration." This goes double for the Jesus Prayer, precisely because it's so soothing.

So we may start by praying fifty knots with our first cup of coffee. Then, after a few months, make it a hundred. Do that for a few more months, and then pray fifty more knots around noon. Eventually we're up to three hundred a day—a hundred in the morning, a hundred at noon, and a hundred in the evening—this is a solid goal. (Some of you will balk at this, but in Russia, many Old Believer peasants pray nine hundred a day!)

Where to pray the Jesus Prayer

The ideal place to pray the Jesus Prayer is a quiet, dimly lit room—somewhere with no distractions. Some people say we should say the prayer with our eyes closed. I like to pray with an icon of Christ or the Holy Family. If you've got access to nature, it's also great to pray this prayer while walking outdoors, as long as you won't be too distracted by other people, road noise, and so forth.

I'm sure you've all heard a Roman Catholic priest say, "If your daily commute is more than ten minutes, you've got time for a daily Rosary." No offense to these good fathers, but I can't stand this idea that prayer is something we can "get out of the way" when we're in the car—especially when it's a meditative prayer like the Rosary.

Likewise, you can spend half an hour every evening saying the Jesus Prayer while you're stuck in traffic driving home from work. And that's great! But if you want the prayer to become a "prayer of the heart," you still have to spend *quality time* with the Jesus Prayer.

That's asking a lot, especially for the mother of small children. The good news is, this is the perfect prayer for busy souls because it can be said with a good deal of compunction while doing ordinary household tasks.

Again, think of the prayer as a conversation with the Lord (because that's what it is). You can't give your full attention to another person while driving—or, if you do, you're not giving your full attention to the road! But you can easily talk to someone while darning a sock or washing dishes. Saint Paisios of Mount Athos recalled his mother saying the Jesus Prayer while kneading bread dough.

Think of the task itself as a timer: "I'll pray the Jesus Prayer for as long as it takes to mop the floor." Just be sure you're not also playing music or watching television. Make sure the task itself isn't too distracting either. You might find it hard to focus on a conversation with Jesus—even in your own heart—while running a vacuum cleaner.

By the way, this works for men too. To quote Saint Paisios:

> I remember a certain worker—John was his name, there on Mount Athos—who worked very hard; he did the work of two men. I had advised him to say the Jesus Prayer while he worked. Gradually, he became accustomed to it. He came to see me once and told me that he felt great joy when he said the Jesus Prayer. "A second dawn is breaking," I told him. After some time I learned that he had been killed by two drunks. Oh, I was so saddened! Some days later, a monk was looking for a tool but couldn't find it because John had put it away somewhere. That night John appeared in the monk's dream and told him where he put the tool.

"You see," the saint explained, "John had attained such a spiritual state that he was able to help others from the life hereafter." Not too shabby.

Using the imagination

Some Western Christians are tempted to treat the Jesus Prayer like a Rosary. They want to picture scenes from Christ's life, or at least Christ Himself. But remember what Saint Heychios said: "Only by means of a mental image can Satan fabricate an evil thought and insinuate this into the intellect in order to lead it astray."

Remember, too, what Metropolitan Kallistos said:

> The Jesus Prayer is not a form of imaginative meditation upon different incidents in the life of Christ. But, while turning aside from images, we are to concentrate our full attention upon, or rather within, the words. The Jesus Prayer is not just a hypnotic incantation but a meaningful phrase, an invocation addressed to another Person. Its object is not relaxation but alertness, not waking slumber but living prayer. And so the Jesus Prayer is not to be said mechanically but with inward purpose; yet at the same time the words should be pronounced without tension, violence, or undue emphasis. The string round our spiritual parcel should be taut, not left hanging slack; yet it should not be drawn so tight as to cut into the edges of the package.

Concentrate your full attention upon, or rather within, the words: that's the best advice I've ever heard on the Jesus Prayer.

St. Joseph the Hesychast likewise urges us:

> Say the prayer "Lord Jesus Christ, have mercy on me" with your tongue and with the nous without ceasing. When the tongue becomes tired let the nous begin. And again, when the nous is burdened, the tongue. Just do not stop. Make many prostrations; keep vigil at night as much as you can.... So then, when praying occupies his nous he

imagines nothing, but pays attention only to the words of
the prayer.

The practitioner *imagines nothing, but pays attention only to the words
of the prayer.*

You might find it better *not* to use the psychosomatic method—
at least at first. The breathing may distract you. That's okay. It's
not about the breathing. It's about being fully present to Christ.
It's about recognizing His presence with (and within!) us.

Weeping during the Jesus Prayer

You might have heard that people weep during the Jesus Prayer.
And you may be wondering, "Should I weep when I pray the Jesus
Prayer? If I don't, am I doing it wrong?"

First of all, never force tears. They are a gift from God. But
the absence of tears should never be cause for discouragement.

Having said that, yes: it's common to weep during the prayer.
Sometimes, the tears we shed are bitter: we're weeping over our
sins. More often, however, they are sweet: we're so overwhelmed
by God's goodness that tears begin to stream down our faces.

But again, *we should neither seek nor expect tears* when saying
the prayer. This is absolutely essential. One of the most common
pitfalls in the spiritual life—and perhaps the most dangerous—is
when we seek a kind of "high" from prayer; in other words, when
we seek consolation, rather than God, in prayer.

This is dangerous, for two reasons. First of all, we can easily
provoke that consolation within ourselves. (Remember the Sufis.)
Secondly, the demons may send us consolation as a form of prelest,
or spiritual delusion.

Ultimately, however, the effect is the same: we become distracted from the true purpose of the prayer, which is to unite

ourselves to Christ. We take something holy and pure and turn it into a toy for spiritual self-pleasuring. Don't do that.

The Jesus Prayer as a "mental health" aid

As long as you set aside time to practice the Jesus Prayer with compunction every day, there's nothing wrong with saying it when (for instance) you're experiencing anxiety or having trouble sleeping.

However, if we *don't* spend time saying the prayer intentionally—if we use it only as a way of relaxing our nerves—it ceases to be a prayer at all and becomes a mantra, a "mindfulness technique."

Choosing a prayer rope

Prayer ropes are also known as *chotki* in Russian and *komboskini* in Greek. That's good to know when you're on the Web trying to buy one. However, unless you're Russian or Greek, please just call it a prayer rope. Please. As I said before, there's no need to make the Jesus Prayer seem alien or exotic.

Now, prayer ropes come in two kinds: Greek and Russian. The Russian-style rope has tassels at the end of the cross; the Greek-style does not. Supposedly the tassels are for drying one's tears. My first prayer rope was a Russian-style but, in my personal experience, they create the *expectation* of tears. For me, they're an invitation to prelest.

Prayer ropes also come in a variety of sizes. Some have 33 knots; some have 100; some have 150; some have 300. A good bet is to buy one that has 100 knots and four beads (i.e., a bead between every 25 knots). This gives you the most flexibility when choosing how many prayers to say.

Buying a prayer rope

Buy your prayer rope from a monastery. Seriously, don't bother with any of the ones you find on Amazon or other online retailers.

Order directly from the monks and nuns. First, it's better to give money to our religious, who give so much to us by their prayers. Secondly, a prayer rope from a monastery will be of higher quality 100 percent of the time. A good prayer rope will last decades, if not a lifetime. A bad prayer rope will last a couple of months, max.

The prayer rope I use comes from Mount Athos (https://www.monastiriaka.gr/en). If you would like something made in the United States, I recommend Saint Paisius Monastery in Safford, Arizona.

Wearing the prayer rope

Christians often wear their prayer ropes wrapped around their left wrists as a reminder to "pray without ceasing." It's also a beautiful public witness to the Christian faith, like wearing a cross outside one's clothing. But while everyone in the West knows what a cross is, hardly anyone knows what a prayer rope is. It's a great conversation starter.

Of course, the prayer rope shouldn't become a mere accessory. As a rule, if you haven't used your rope in the last twenty-four hours, you shouldn't wear it.

In conclusion

I'll give the last word to Saint Theophan the Recluse, perhaps the greatest master of the Jesus Prayer in modern times:

> The various methods described by the Fathers (sitting down, making prostrations, and the other techniques used when performing this prayer) are not suitable for everyone: indeed without a personal director they are actually dangerous. It is better not to try them. There is just one method which is obligatory for all: *to stand with attention in the heart.*

All other things are beside the point and do not lead to the crux of the matter.

It is said of the fruit of this prayer, that there is nothing higher in the world. This is wrong. As if it were some talisman! Nothing in the words of the prayer and their uttering can alone bring forth its fruit. All fruit can be received without this prayer, and even without any oral prayer, but merely by directing the mind and heart toward God.

The essence of the whole thing is to be established in the remembrance of God, and to walk into his presence. You can say to anyone: "Follow whatever method you like—recite the Jesus Prayer, perform bows and prostrations, go to Church: do what you wish, only strive to be always in constant remembrance of God."

Appendix B

A Guide to Street Evangelism

1. Never evangelize alone or in a group larger than three. Going alone can be dangerous, but going in large groups can make the "evangelizees" feel overwhelmed or ganged up on.

2. Dress neatly and modestly, but don't be excessively formal. Avoid T-shirts with cheesy religious slogans, hoodies with graphic "memento mori" skulls, and so forth. You don't want to mark yourself out as belonging to a certain subculture.

3. Set up on a busy street corner. Have the following items:
   - a folding table
   - an eye-catching image of religious significance: a sign, a banner, an icon, or the like
   - literature or holy cards, or both, that passersby can take
   - a prayer aid: rosary beads, a prayer rope, a pocket Bible, and so forth

4. Don't be upset if folks accept your swag without stopping to talk. Evangelists give away swag for the same reason TD Bank gives away pens. Every time someone looks at the rosary or the

holy card, he'll think of you—and, more importantly, of God. That memento could bear fruit hours, days, or even years later.

5. Don't try to stop people and talk to them about Jesus. Instead, smile at them and make eye contact. If they're curious, they'll stop and ask what you're all about. Better yet, keep a cooler full of bottles of ice water and simply hand them out. A small act of kindness may open their hearts.

6. Be prepared to offer an "elevator pitch" for Christianity if someone stops. For instance: "We believe that God created the world in love, but that man fell into sin. Yet God loves us so much that He sent His only Son to die for our sins. But Christ rose from the dead, and He offers eternal life to everyone, if only we live as He lived and love as He loved."

7. Bring sandwiches and cigarettes. Throw them in a backpack with some water bottles. Take a walk and hand out the food to any homeless folks you come across. Don't try to convert them, but if they ask who you are and what you're doing, tell them. Again, the act of kindness simply gives God an opportunity to open their hearts. But if and when He does, be ready.

8. Be present to people. Whatever the person in front of you has to say, listen—within reason, of course. Remember what Saint John says: "Beloved, let us love one another, for love is of God; and everyone who loves is born of God and knows God. He who does not love does not know God, for God is love" (1 John 4:7–8). Spending time with the lonely (and who in the world today isn't lonely?) is a work of mercy in itself. But because God is love, this encounter with love—the love you're showing them—is truly an encounter with God. And, again, that single moment of contact may change someone's whole life. That person may look back ten years from now and say, "That was the day I met Him."

Appendix C

The *Didache*

1. The Two Ways; the First Commandment

There are two ways, one of life and one of death; but a great difference between the two ways. The way of life, then, is this: First, you shall love God who made you; second, your neighbour as yourself; and all things whatsoever you would should not occur to you, do not also do to another. And of these sayings the teaching is this: Bless those who curse you, and pray for your enemies, and fast for those who persecute you. For what reward is there, if you love those who love you? Do not also the Gentiles do the same? But love those who hate you, and you shall not have an enemy. Abstain from fleshly and worldly lusts. If someone gives you a blow upon your right cheek, turn to him the other also, and you shall be perfect. If someone impresses you for one mile, go with him two. If someone takes away your cloak, give him also your coat. If someone takes from you what is yours, ask it not back, for indeed you are not able. Give to every one that asks you, and ask it not back; for the Father wills that to all should be given of our own blessings (free gifts). Happy is he that gives according to the commandment; for he is guiltless. Woe to him that receives; for if one having need receives, he is guiltless; but he that receives not having need, shall pay the penalty, why he received and for what, and, coming into straits (confinement), he shall be examined concerning the things which he has done, and he shall not escape thence until he pay back the last farthing (Matt. 5:26). But also now concerning this, it has been said, Let your alms sweat in your hands, until you know to whom you should give.

2. The Second Commandment: Gross Sin Forbidden

And the second commandment of the Teaching; You shall not commit murder, you shall not commit adultery (Exod. 20:13–14), you shall not commit pederasty, you shall not commit fornication, you shall not steal (Exod. 20:15), you shall not practice magic, you shall not practice witchcraft, you shall not murder a child by abortion nor kill that which is begotten. You shall not covet the things of your neighbour (Exod. 20:17), you shall not forswear yourself, (Matt. 5:34), you shall not bear false witness (Exod. 20:16), you shall not speak evil, you shall bear no grudge. You shall not be double-minded nor double-tongued; for to be double-tongued is a snare of death. Your speech shall not be false, nor empty, but fulfilled by deed. You shall not be covetous, nor rapacious, nor a hypocrite, nor evil disposed, nor haughty. You shall not take evil counsel against your neighbour. You shall not hate any man; but some you shall reprove, and concerning some you shall pray, and some you shall love more than your own life.

3. Other Sins Forbidden

My child, flee from every evil thing, and from every likeness of it. Be not prone to anger, for anger leads the way to murder; neither jealous, nor quarrelsome, nor of hot temper; for out of all these murders are engendered. My child, be not a lustful one; for lust leads the way to fornication; neither a filthy talker, nor of lofty eye; for out of all these adulteries are engendered. My child, be not an observer of omens, since it leads the way to idolatry; neither an enchanter, nor an astrologer, nor a purifier, nor be willing to look at these things; for out of all these idolatry is engendered. My child, be not a liar, since a lie leads the way to theft; neither money-loving, nor vainglorious, for out of all these thefts are engendered. My child, be not a murmurer, since it leads the way to blasphemy; neither self-willed nor evil-minded, for out of all these blasphemies are engendered. But be meek, since the meek shall inherit the earth (Matt. 5:5). Be long-suffering and pitiful and guileless and gentle and good and always trembling at the words which you have heard. You shall not exalt yourself (Luke 18:14), nor give overconfidence to your soul. Your soul shall not be joined with lofty ones, but with just and lowly ones shall it have its intercourse. The workings that befall you receive as good, knowing that apart from God nothing comes to pass.

4. Various Precepts

My child, him that speaks to you the word of God remember night and day; and you shall honour him as the Lord; for in the place whence lordly rule is uttered, there is the Lord. And you shall seek out day by day the faces of the saints, in order that you may rest upon their words. You shall not long for division, but shall bring those who contend to peace. You shall judge righteously, you shall not respect persons in reproving for transgressions. You shall not be undecided whether it shall be or no. Be not a stretcher forth of the hands to receive and a drawer of them back to give. If you have anything, through your hands you shall give ransom for your sins. You shall not hesitate to give, nor murmur when you give; for you shall know who is the good repayer of the hire. You shall not turn away from him that is in want, but you shall share all things with your brother, and shall not say that they are your own; for if you are partakers in that which is immortal, how much more in things which are mortal? You shall not remove your hand from your son or from your daughter, but from their youth shall teach them the fear of God (Eph. 6:4). You shall not enjoin anything in your bitterness upon your bondman or maidservant, who hope in the same God, lest ever they shall fear not God who is over both (Eph. 6:9; Col. 4:1); for he comes not to call according to the outward appearance, but unto them whom the Spirit has prepared. And you bondmen shall be subject to your masters as to a type of God, in modesty and fear (Eph. 6:5; Col. 3:22). You shall hate all hypocrisy and everything which is not pleasing to the Lord. Forsake in no way the commandments of the Lord; but you shall keep what you have received, neither adding thereto nor taking away therefrom (Deut. 12:32). In the church you shall acknowledge your transgressions, and you shall not come near for your prayer with an evil conscience. This is the way of life.

5. The Way of Death

And the way of death is this: First of all it is evil and full of curse: murders, adulteries, lusts, fornications, thefts, idolatries, magic arts, witchcrafts, rapines, false witnessings, hypocrisies, double-heartedness, deceit, haughtiness, depravity, self-will, greediness, filthy talking, jealousy, overconfidence, loftiness, boastfulness; persecutors of the good, hating truth, loving a lie, not knowing a reward for righteousness, not cleaving to good nor to righteous judgment, watching not for that which is good, but for that which is evil; from whom meekness and endurance are far, loving vanities, pursuing requital, not pitying a poor man, not labouring for the afflicted, not knowing Him that made them, murderers of children, destroyers of the handiwork of God, turning away from him that is in want, afflicting him that is distressed, advocates of the rich, lawless judges of the poor, utter sinners. Be delivered, children, from all these.

6. Against False Teachers, and Food Offered to Idols

See that no one cause you to err from this way of the Teaching, since apart from God it teaches you. For if you are able to bear all the yoke of the Lord, you will be perfect; but if you are not able, do what you are able. And concerning food, bear what you are able; but against that which is sacrificed to idols be exceedingly on your guard; for it is the service of dead gods.

7. Concerning Baptism

And concerning baptism, baptize this way: Having first said all these things, baptize into the name of the Father, and of the Son, and of the Holy Spirit (Matt. 28:19), in living water. But if you have not living water, baptize into other water; and if you cannot in cold, in warm. But if you have not either, pour out water thrice upon the head in the name of Father and Son and Holy Spirit. But before the baptism let the baptizer fast, and the baptized, and whatever others can; but you shall order the baptized to fast one or two days before.

8. Concerning Fasting and Prayer

But let not your fasts be with the hypocrites (Matt. 6:16), for they fast on the second and fifth day of the week; but fast on the fourth day and the Preparation (Friday). Neither pray as the hypocrites; but as the Lord commanded in His Gospel, thus pray: Our Father who art in heaven, hallowed be Your name. Your kingdom come. Your will be done, as in heaven, so on earth. Give us today our daily (needful) bread, and forgive us our debt as we also forgive our debtors. And bring us not into temptation, but deliver us from the evil one (or, evil); for Yours is the power and the glory forever. Thrice in the day thus pray.

9. The Thanksgiving

Now concerning the Thanksgiving [*eucharistía*; eucharist], thus give thanks. First, concerning the cup: We thank You, our Father, for the holy vine of David Your servant, which You made known to us through Jesus Your Servant; to You be the glory forever. And concerning the broken bread: We thank You, our Father, for the life and knowledge which You made known to us through Jesus Your Servant; to You be the glory forever. Even as this broken bread was scattered over the hills, and was gathered together and became one, so let Your Church be gathered together from the ends of the earth into Your kingdom; for Yours is the glory and the power through Jesus Christ forever. But let no one eat or drink of your Thanksgiving, but they who have been baptized into the name of the Lord; for concerning this also the Lord has said, Give not that which is holy to the dogs (Matt. 7:6).

10. Prayer after Communion

But after you are filled, thus give thanks: We thank You, holy Father, for Your holy name which You caused to tabernacle in our hearts, and for the knowledge and faith and immortality, which You made known to us through Jesus Your Servant; to You be the glory forever. You, Master almighty, created all things for Your name's sake; You gave food and drink to men for enjoyment, that they might give thanks to You; but to us You freely gave spiritual food and drink and life eternal through Your Servant. Before all things we thank You that You are mighty; to You be the glory forever. Remember, Lord, Your Church, to deliver it from all evil and to make it perfect in Your love, and gather it from the four winds, sanctified for Your kingdom which You have prepared for it; for Yours is the power and the glory forever. Let grace come, and let this world pass away. Hosanna to the God (Son) of David! If any one is holy, let him come; if any one is not so, let him repent. Maranatha. Amen. But permit the prophets to make Thanksgiving as much as they desire.

11. Concerning Teachers, Apostles, and Prophets

Whosoever, therefore, comes and teaches you all these things that have been said before, receive him. But if the teacher himself turn and teach another doctrine to the destruction of this, hear him not; but if he teach so as to increase righteousness and the knowledge of the Lord, receive him as the Lord. But concerning the apostles and prophets, according to the decree of the Gospel, thus do. Let every apostle that comes to you be received as the Lord. But he shall not remain except one day; but if there be need, also the next; but if he remain three days, he is a false prophet. And when the apostle goes away, let him take nothing but bread until he lodges; but if he ask money, he is a false prophet. And every prophet that speaks in the Spirit you shall neither try nor judge; for every sin shall be forgiven, but this sin shall not be forgiven. But not every one that speaks in the Spirit is a prophet; but only if he hold the ways of the Lord. Therefore from their ways shall the false prophet and the prophet be known. And every prophet who orders a meal in the Spirit eats not from it, except indeed he be a false prophet; and every prophet who teaches the truth, if he do not what he teaches, is a false prophet. And every prophet, proved true, working unto the mystery of the Church in the world, yet not teaching others to do what he himself does, shall not be judged among you, for with God he has his judgment; for so did also the ancient prophets. But whoever says in the Spirit, Give me money, or something else, you shall not listen to him; but if he says to you to give for others' sake who are in need, let no one judge him.

12. Reception of Christians

But let every one that comes in the name of the Lord be received, and afterward you shall prove and know him; for you shall have understanding right and left. If he who comes is a wayfarer, assist him as far as you are able; but he shall not remain with you, except for two or three days, if need be. But if he wills to abide with you, being an artisan, let him work and eat (2 Thess. 3:10); but if he has no trade, according to your understanding see to it that, as a Christian, he shall not live with you idle. But if he wills not to do, he is a Christ-monger. Watch that you keep aloof from such.

13. Support of Prophets

But every true prophet that wills to abide among you is worthy of his support. So also a true teacher is himself worthy, as the work-man, of his support (Matt. 10:10; cf. Luke 10:7). Every first-fruit, therefore, of the products of wine-press and threshing-floor, of oxen and of sheep, you shall take and give to the prophets, for they are your high priests. But if you have not a prophet, give it to the poor. If you make a batch of dough, take the first-fruit and give according to the commandment. So also when you open a jar of wine or of oil, take the first-fruit and give it to the prophets; and of money (silver) and clothing and every possession, take the first-fruit, as it may seem good to you, and give according to the commandment.

14. Christian Assembly on the Lord's Day

But every Lord's day gather yourselves together, and break bread, and give thanksgiving after having confessed your transgressions, that your sacrifice may be pure. But let no one that is at variance with his fellow come together with you, until they be reconciled, that your sacrifice may not be profaned. For this is that which was spoken by the Lord: In every place and time offer to me a pure sacrifice; for I am a great King, says the Lord, and my name is wonderful among the nations.

15. Bishops and Deacons; Christian Reproof

Therefore, appoint for yourselves bishops and deacons worthy of the Lord, men meek, and not lovers of money (1 Tim. 3:4), and truthful and proven; for they also render to you the service of prophets and teachers. Despise them not therefore, for they are your honoured ones, together with the prophets and teachers. And reprove one another, not in anger, but in peace, as you have it in the Gospel (Matt. 18:15–17); but to every one that acts amiss against another, let no one speak, nor let him hear anything from you until he repents. But your prayers and alms and all your deeds so do, as you have it in the Gospel of our Lord.

16. Watchfulness; the Coming of the Lord

Watch for your life's sake. Let not your lamps be quenched, nor your loins unloosed; but be ready, for you know not the hour in which our Lord comes (Matt. 24:42). But often shall you come together, seeking the things which are befitting to your souls: for the whole time of your faith will not profit you, if you be not made perfect in the last time. For in the last days false prophets and corrupters shall be multiplied, and the sheep shall be turned into wolves, and love shall be turned into hate (Matt. 24:11–12); for when lawlessness increases, they shall hate and persecute and betray one another (Matt. 24:10), and then shall appear the world-deceiver as the Son of God, and shall do signs and wonders, and the earth shall be delivered into his hands, and he shall do iniquitous things which have never yet come to pass since the beginning. Then shall the creation of men come into the fire of trial, and many shall be made to stumble and shall perish; but they that endure in their faith shall be saved from under the curse itself. And then shall appear the signs of the truth; first, the sign of an outspreading in heaven; then the sign of the sound of the trumpet; and the third, the resurrection of the dead; yet not of all, but as it is said: The Lord shall come and all His saints with Him. Then shall the world see the Lord coming upon the clouds of heaven.

The *Epistle to Diognetus*

1. Occasion of the Epistle

Most excellent Diognetus,

I can see that you deeply desire to learn how Christians worship their God. You have so carefully and earnestly asked your questions about them: What is it about the God they believe in, and the form of religion they observe, that lets them look down upon the world and despise death? Why do they reject the Greek gods and the Jewish superstitions alike? What about the affection they all have for each other? And why has this new group and their practices come to life only now, and not long ago?

I cordially welcome this desire of yours, and I implore God, who enables us both to speak and to hear, to grant to me so to speak, that, above all, I may hear you have been edified, and to you so to hear, that I who speak may have no cause of regret for having done so.

2. The Vanity of Idols

Come, then, after you have freed yourself from all prejudices possessing your mind, and laid aside what you have been accustomed to, as something apt to deceive you, and being made, as if from the beginning, a new man, inasmuch as, according to your own confession, you are to be the hearer of a new system of doctrine; come and contemplate, not with your eyes only, but with your understanding, the substance and the form of those whom you declare and deem to be gods.

Is not one of them a stone similar to that on which we tread? Is not a second brass, in no way superior to those vessels which are constructed for our ordinary use? Is not a third wood, and that already rotten? Is not a fourth silver, which needs a man to watch it, lest it be stolen? Is not a fifth iron, consumed by rust? Is not a sixth earthenware, in no degree more valuable than that which is formed for the humblest purposes?

Are not all these of corruptible matter? Are they not fabricated by means of iron and fire? Did not the sculptor fashion one of them, the brazier a second, the silversmith a third, and the potter a fourth? Was not every one of them, before they were formed by the arts of these workmen into the shape of these gods, each in its own way subject to change? Would not those things which are now vessels, formed of the same materials, become like to such, if they met with the same artificers? Might not these, which are now worshipped by you, again be made by men vessels similar to others? Are they not all deaf? Are they not blind? Are they not without life? Are they not destitute of feeling? Are they not incapable of motion? Are they not all prone to decay? Are they not all corruptible?

These things you call gods; these you serve; these you worship; and you become altogether like them. For this reason you hate the Christians, because they do not deem *these* to be gods. But do not you yourselves, who now think and suppose such to be gods, much more cast contempt upon them than they the Christians do? Do you not much more mock and insult them, when you worship those that are made of stone and earthenware, without appointing any persons to guard them; but those made of silver and gold you shut up by night, and appoint watchers to look after them by day, lest they be stolen? And by those gifts which you mean to present to them, do you not, if they are possessed of sense, rather punish than honour them? But if, on the other hand, they are destitute of sense, you convict them of this fact, while you worship them with blood and the smoke of sacrifices. Let any one of you suffer such indignities! Let any one of you endure to have such things done to himself! But not a single human being will, unless compelled to it, endure such treatment, since he is endowed with sense and reason. A stone, however, readily bears it, seeing it is insensible. Certainly you do not show by your conduct that he your God is possessed of sense. And as to the fact that Christians are not accustomed to serve such gods, I might easily find many other things to say; but if even what has been said does not seem to any one sufficient, I deem it idle to say anything further.

3. Superstitions of the Jews

And next, I imagine that you are most desirous of hearing something on this point, that the Christians do not observe the same forms of divine worship as do the Jews. The Jews, then, if they abstain from the kind of service above described, and deem it proper to worship one God as being Lord of all, are right; but if they offer Him worship in the way which we have described, they greatly err. For while the Gentiles, by offering such things to those that are destitute of sense and hearing, furnish an example of madness; they, on the other hand by thinking to offer these things to God as if He needed them, might justly reckon it rather an act of folly than of divine worship. For He that made heaven and earth, and all that is therein, and gives to us all the things of which we stand in need, certainly requires none of those things which He Himself bestows on such as think of furnishing them to Him. But those who imagine that, by means of blood, and the smoke of sacrifices and burnt-offerings, they offer sacrifices acceptable to Him, and that by such honours they show Him respect — these, by supposing that they can give anything to Him who needs nothing, appear to me in no respect to differ from those who studiously confer the same honour on things destitute of sense, and which therefore are unable to enjoy such honours.

4. The Other Observances of the Jews

But as to their scrupulosity concerning food, and their superstition as respects the Sabbaths, and their boasting about circumcision, and their fancies about fasting and the new moons, which are utterly ridiculous and unworthy of notice — I do not think that you require to learn anything from me. For, to accept some of those things which have been formed by God for the use of men as properly formed, and to reject others as useless and redundant — how can this be lawful? And to speak falsely of God, as if He forbade us to do what is good on the Sabbath-days — how is not this impious? And to glory in the circumcision of the flesh as a proof of election, and as if, on account of it, they were specially beloved by God — how is it not a subject of ridicule? And as to their observing months and days (Gal. 4:10), as if waiting upon the stars and the moon, and their distributing, according to their own tendencies, the appointments of God, and the vicissitudes of the seasons, some for festivities, and others for mourning — who would deem this a part of divine worship, and not much rather a manifestation of folly? I suppose, then, you are sufficiently convinced that the Christians properly abstain from the vanity and error common to both Jews and Gentiles, and from the busybody spirit and vain boasting of the Jews; but you must not hope to learn the mystery of their peculiar mode of worshipping God from any mortal.

5. The Manners of the Christians

For the Christians are distinguished from other men neither by country, nor language, nor the customs which they observe. For they neither inhabit cities of their own, nor employ a peculiar form of speech, nor lead a life which is marked out by any singularity. The course of conduct which they follow has not been devised by any speculation or deliberation of inquisitive men; nor do they, like some, proclaim themselves the advocates of any merely human doctrines. But, inhabiting Greek as well as barbarian cities, according as the lot of each of them has determined, and following the customs of the natives in respect to clothing, food, and the rest of their ordinary conduct, they display to us their wonderful and confessedly striking method of life. They dwell in their own countries, but simply as sojourners. As citizens, they share in all things with others, and yet endure all things as if foreigners. Every foreign land is to them as their native country, and every land of their birth as a land of strangers. They marry, as do all others; they beget children; but they do not destroy their offspring. They have a common table, but not a common bed. They are in the flesh, but they do not live after the flesh (2 Cor. 10:3). They pass their days on earth, but they are citizens of heaven (Phil. 3:20). They obey the prescribed laws, and at the same time surpass the laws by their lives. They love all men, and are persecuted by all. They are unknown and condemned; they are put to death, and restored to life (2 Cor. 6:9). They are poor, yet make many rich (2 Cor. 6:10); they are in lack of all things, and yet abound in all; they are dishonoured, and yet in their very dishonour are glorified. They are evil spoken of, and yet are justified; they are reviled, and bless (2 Cor. 4:12); they are insulted, and repay the insult with honour; they do good, yet are punished as evil-doers. When punished, they rejoice as if quickened into life; they are assailed by the Jews as foreigners, and are persecuted by the Greeks; yet those who hate them are unable to assign any reason for their hatred.

6. The Relation of Christians to the World

To sum up all in one word—what the soul is in the body, Christians are in the world. The soul is dispersed through all the members of the body, and Christians are scattered through all the cities of the world. The soul dwells in the body, yet is not of the body; and Christians dwell in the world, yet are not of the world. The invisible soul is guarded by the visible body, and Christians are known indeed to be in the world, but their godliness remains invisible. The flesh hates the soul, and wars against it (1 Pet. 2:11), though itself suffering no injury, because it is prevented from enjoying pleasures; the world also hates the Christians, though in no wise injured, because they abjure pleasures. The soul loves the flesh that hates it, and loves also the members; Christians likewise love those that hate them. The soul is imprisoned in the body, yet keeps together that very body; and Christians are confined in the world as in a prison, and yet they keep together the world. The immortal soul dwells in a mortal tabernacle; and Christians dwell as sojourners in corruptible bodies, looking for an incorruptible dwelling in the heavens. The soul, when but ill-provided with food and drink, becomes better; in like manner, the Christians, though subjected day by day to punishment, increase the more in number. God has assigned them this illustrious position, which it were unlawful for them to forsake.

7. The Manifestation of Christ

For, as I said, this was no mere earthly invention which was delivered to them, nor is it a mere human system of opinion, which they judge it right to preserve so carefully, nor has a dispensation of mere human mysteries been committed to them, but truly God Himself, who is almighty, the Creator of all things, and invisible, has sent from heaven, and placed among men, Him who is the truth, and the holy and incomprehensible Word, and has firmly established Him in their hearts. He did not, as one might have imagined, send to men any servant, or angel, or ruler, or any one of those who bear sway over earthly things, or one of those to whom the government of things in the heavens has been entrusted, but the very Creator and Fashioner of all things—by whom He made the heavens—by whom he enclosed the sea within its proper bounds—whose ordinances all the stars faithfully observe—from whom the sun has received the measure of his daily course to be observed—whom the moon obeys, being commanded to shine in the night, and whom the stars also obey, following the moon in her course; by whom all things have been arranged, and placed within their proper limits, and to whom all are subject—the heavens and the things that are therein, the earth and the things that are therein, the sea and the things that are therein—fire, air, and the abyss—the things which are in the heights, the things which are in the depths, and the things which lie between. This messenger He sent to them. Was it then, as one might conceive, for the purpose of exercising tyranny, or of inspiring fear and terror? By no means, but under the influence of clemency and meekness. As a king sends his son, who is also a king, so sent He Him; as God He sent Him; as to men He sent Him; as a Saviour He sent Him, and as seeking to persuade, not to compel us; for violence has no place in the character of God. As calling us He sent Him, not as vengefully pursuing us; as loving us He sent Him, not as judging us. For He will yet send Him to judge us, and who shall endure His appearing? (Mal. 3:2).

[*A considerable gap here occurs in the manuscripts.*]

Do you not see them exposed to wild beasts, that they may be persuaded to deny the Lord, and yet not overcome? Do you not see that the more of them are punished, the greater becomes the number of the rest? This does not seem to be the work of man: this is the power of God; these are the evidences of His manifestation.

8. The Miserable State of Men before the Coming of the Word

For, who of men at all understood before His coming what God is? Do you accept of the vain and silly doctrines of those who are deemed trustworthy philosophers? Of whom some said that fire was God, calling that God to which they themselves were by and by to come; and some water; and others some other of the elements formed by God. But if any one of these theories be worthy of approbation, every one of the rest of created things might also be declared to be God. But such declarations are simply the startling and erroneous utterances of deceivers; and no man has either seen Him, or made Him known, but He has revealed Himself. And He has manifested Himself through faith, to which alone it is given to behold God. For God, the Lord and Fashioner of all things, who made all things, and assigned them their several positions, proved Himself not merely a friend of mankind, but also long-suffering in His dealings with them. Yea, He was always of such a character, and still is, and will ever be, kind and good, and free from wrath, and true, and the only one who is absolutely good (Matt. 19:17); and He formed in His mind a great and unspeakable conception, which He communicated to His Son alone. As long, then, as He held and preserved His own wise counsel in concealment, He appeared to neglect us, and to have no care over us. But after He revealed and laid open, through His beloved Son, the things which had been prepared from the beginning, He conferred every blessing all at once upon us, so that we should both share in His benefits, and see and be active in His service. Who of us would ever have expected these things? He was aware, then, of all things in His own mind, along with His Son, according to the relation subsisting between them.

9. Why the Son Was Sent So Late

As long then as the former time endured, He permitted us to be borne along by unruly impulses, being drawn away by the desire of pleasure and various lusts. This was not that He at all delighted in our sins, but that He simply endured them; nor that He approved the time of working iniquity which then was, but that He sought to form a mind conscious of righteousness, so that being convinced in that time of our unworthiness of attaining life through our own works, it should now, through the kindness of God, be vouchsafed to us; and having made it manifest that in ourselves we were unable to enter into the kingdom of God, we might through the power of God be made able. But when our wickedness had reached its height, and it had been clearly shown that its reward, punishment and death, was impending over us; and when the time had come which God had before appointed for manifesting His own kindness and power, how the one love of God, through exceeding regard for men, did not regard us with hatred, nor thrust us away, nor remember our iniquity against us, but showed great long-suffering, and bore with us, He Himself took on Him the burden of our iniquities, He gave His own Son as a ransom for us, the holy One for transgressors, the blameless One for the wicked, the righteous One for the unrighteous, the incorruptible One for the corruptible, the immortal One for those who are mortal. For what other thing was capable of covering our sins than His righteousness? By what other one was it possible that we, the wicked and ungodly, could be justified, than by the only Son of God? O sweet exchange! O unsearchable operation! O benefits surpassing all expectation! That the wickedness of many should be hid in a single righteous One, and that the righteousness of One should justify many transgressors! Having therefore convinced us in the former time that our nature was unable to attain to life, and having now revealed the Saviour who is able to save even those things which it was formerly impossible to save, by both these facts He desired to lead us to trust in His kindness, to esteem Him our Nourisher, Father, Teacher, Counsellor, Healer, our Wisdom, Light, Honour, Glory, Power, and Life, so that we should not be anxious concerning clothing and food.

10. The Blessings That Will Flow from Faith

If you also desire to possess this faith, you likewise shall receive first of all the knowledge of the Father. For God has loved mankind, on whose account He made the world, to whom He rendered subject all the things that are in it, to whom He gave reason and understanding, to whom alone He imparted the privilege of look-ing upwards to Himself, whom He formed after His own image, to whom He sent His only-begotten Son, to whom He has promised a kingdom in heaven, and will give it to those who have loved Him. And when you have attained this knowledge, with what joy do you think you will be filled? Or, how will you love Him who has first so loved you? And if you love Him, you will be an imitator of His kindness. And do not wonder that a man may become an imita-tor of God. He can, if he is willing. For it is not by ruling over his neighbours, or by seeking to hold the supremacy over those that

are weaker, or by being rich, and showing violence towards those
that are inferior, that happiness is found; nor can any one by these
things become an imitator of God. But these things do not at all
constitute His majesty. On the contrary he who takes upon himself
the burden of his neighbour; he who, in whatsoever respect he
may be superior, is ready to benefit another who is deficient; he
who, whatsoever things he has received from God, by distributing these to the needy, becomes a god to those who receive his
benefits: he is an imitator of God. Then you shall see, while still
on earth, that God in the heavens rules over the universe; then
you shall begin to speak the mysteries of God; then shall you both
love and admire those that suffer punishment because they will
not deny God; then shall you condemn the deceit and error of the
world when you shall know what it is to live truly in heaven, when
you shall despise that which is here esteemed to be death, when
you shall fear what is truly death, which is reserved for those who
shall be condemned to the eternal fire, which shall afflict those
even to the end that are committed to it. Then shall you admire
those who for righteousness' sake endure the fire that is but for a
moment, and shall count them happy when you shall know the
nature of that fire.

11. These Things Are Worthy to Be Known and Believed

I do not speak of things strange to me, nor do I aim at anything
inconsistent with right reason; but having been a disciple of the
Apostles, I have become a teacher of the Gentiles. I minister the
things delivered to me to those that are disciples worthy of the
truth. For who that is rightly taught and begotten by the loving
Word, would not seek to learn accurately the things which have
been clearly shown by the Word to His disciples, to whom the
Word being manifested has revealed them, speaking plainly to

them, not understood indeed by the unbelieving, but conversing with the disciples, who, being esteemed faithful by Him, acquired a knowledge of the mysteries of the Father? For which reason He sent the Word, that He might be manifested to the world; and He, being despised by the people of the Jews, was, when preached by the Apostles, believed in by the Gentiles. This is He who was from the beginning, who appeared as if new, and was found old, and yet who is ever born afresh in the hearts of the saints. This is He who, being from everlasting, is today called the Son; through whom the Church is enriched, and grace, widely spread, increases in the saints, furnishing understanding, revealing mysteries, announcing times, rejoicing over the faithful, giving to those that seek, by whom the limits of faith are not broken through, nor the boundaries set by the fathers passed over. Then the fear of the law is chanted, and the grace of the prophets is known, and the faith of the gospels is established, and the tradition of the Apostles is preserved, and the grace of the Church exults; which grace if you grieve not, you shall know those things which the Word teaches, by whom He wills, and when He pleases. For whatever things we are moved to utter by the will of the Word commanding us, we communicate to you with pains, and from a love of the things that have been revealed to us.

12. The Importance of Knowledge to True Spiritual Life

When you have read and carefully listened to these things, you shall know what God bestows on such as rightly love Him, being made as you are a paradise of delight, presenting in yourselves a tree bearing all kinds of produce and flourishing well, being adorned with various fruits. For in this place the tree of knowledge and the tree of life have been planted; but it is not the tree of knowledge that destroys — it is disobedience that proves destructive. Nor truly are those words without significance which are written, how God from the beginning planted the tree of life in the midst of paradise, revealing through knowledge the way to life, and when those who were first formed did not use this knowledge properly, they were, through the fraud of the Serpent, stripped naked. For neither can life exist without knowledge, nor is knowledge secure without life. Wherefore both were planted close together. The Apostle, perceiving the force of this conjunction, and blaming that knowledge which, without true doctrine, is admitted to influence life, declares: Knowledge puffs up, but love edifies. For he who thinks he knows anything without true knowledge, and such as is witnessed to by life, knows nothing, but is deceived by the Serpent, as not loving life. But he who combines knowledge with fear, and seeks after life, plants in hope, looking for fruit. Let your heart be your wisdom; and let your life be true knowledge inwardly received. Bearing this tree and displaying its fruit, you shall always gather in those things which are desired by God, which the Serpent cannot reach, and to which deception does not approach; nor is Eve then corrupted, but is trusted as a virgin; and salvation is manifested, and the Apostles are filled with understanding, and the Passover of the Lord advances, and the choirs are gathered together, and are arranged in proper order, and the Word rejoices in teaching the saints—by whom the Father is glorified: to whom be glory forever. Amen.

Bibliography

Augustine. *The City of God*. New York: Modern Library, 1993.

———. *Essential Sermons*. Hyde Park: New City Press, 2007.

Bloom, Anthony. *Churchianity vs Christianity*. Yonkers, NY: St. Vladimir's Seminary Press, 2017.

Chaput, Charles. *Strangers in a Strange Land: Living the Catholic Faith in a Post-Christian World*. New York: Henry Holt, 2017.

Dreher, Rod. *The Benedict Option*. New York: Sentinel, 2018.

———. *Live Not by Lies*. New York: Sentinel, 2020.

Eliot, T. S. *Christianity and Culture: Essays*. New York: Mariner, 1960.

Farasiotis, Dionysios. *The Gurus, the Young Man, and Elder Paisios*. Platina, CA: St. Herman of Alaska Brotherhood, 2008.

Francis. *Evangelii Gaudium: The Joy of the Gospel*. New York: Image, 2014.

Hart, David Bentley. *The Beauty of the Infinite: The Aesthetics of Christian Truth*. Grand Rapids: Eerdmans, 2004.

Heine, Ronald E. *Origen: An Introduction to His Life and Thought*. Eugene. OR: Cascade, 2019.

Holland, Tom. *Dominion: How the Christian Revolution Remade the World*. New York: Basic Books, 2019.

Igumen Chariton. *The Art of Prayer: An Orthodox Anthology*. New York: Farrar, Straus and Giroux, 1997.

Lewis, C. S. *Mere Christianity*. New York: HarperOne, 2009.

———. *Present Concerns: Journalistic Essays*. New York: HarperOne, 2017.

MacDonald, George. *Creation in Christ: Unspoken Sermons*. Vancouver: Regent College Publishing, 2004.

MacIntyre, Alasdair. *After Virtue: A Study in Moral Theory*. South Bend, IN: Notre Dame University Press, 2007.

Makhlouf, Charbel, and Hanna Skandar. *Love Is a Radiant Light: The Life and Words of Saint Charbel*. Translated by William J. Melcher. Brooklyn: Angelico Press, 2019.

Maritain, Jacques. *The Primacy of the Spiritual: On Those Things Which Are Not Caesar's*. Providence: Cluny Media, 2020.

Newman, John Henry. *Parochial and Plain Sermons*. San Francisco: Ignatius Press, 1997.

Paisios of Mount Athos. *Spiritual Counsels, Volume IV: Family Life*. Edited by Anna Famellos. Translated by Father Peter Chamberas. Thessaloniki: Holy Hesychaterion "Evangelist John the Theologian," 2022.

Péguy, Charles. *Temporal and Eternal*. Carmel: Liberty Fund, 2001.

The Philokalia, Vols. I and IV. London: Faber & Faber, 1979.

Ratzinger, Joseph. *Salt of the Earth: The Church at the end of the Millennium*. San Francisco: Ignatius Press, 1997.

———. *Without Roots: The West, Relativism, Christianity, Islam*. New York: Basic Books, 2007.

Rose, Seraphim. *Orthodoxy and the Religion of the Future*. Platina, CA: St. Herman of Alaska Brotherhood, 1997.

Schmemann, Alexander. *For the Life of the World: Sacraments and Orthodoxy*. Yonkers, NY: St. Vladimir's Seminary Press, 2018.

——. *Great Lent: Journey to Pascha.* Yonkers, NY: St. Vladimir's Seminary Press, 1974.

Schuon, Frithjof. *The Essential Frithjof Schuon.* Edited by Seyyed Hossein Nasr. Bloomington, IN: World Wisdom, 2005.

Sherrard, Philip. *Christianity: Linaments of a Sacred Tradition.* Brookline, MA: Holy Cross Orthodox Press, 2017.

Stark, Rodney. *The Rise of Christianity: A Sociologist Reconsiders History.* Princeton: Princeton University Press, 2023.

Strickland, John. *The Age of Paradise: Christendom from Pentecost to the First Millennium.* Chesterton, IN: Ancient Faith Publishing, 2019.

Ware, Kallistos. *The Orthodox Church.* New York: Penguin, 2015.

——. *The Orthodox Way.* Yonkers, NY: St. Vladimir's Seminary Press, 2019.

Webber, Meletios. *Bread and Water, Wine and Oil.* Chesterton, IN: Ancient Faith Publishing, 2007.

Yannoulatos, Anastasios. *Mission in Christ's Way: An Orthodox Understanding of Mission.* Brookline, MA: Holy Cross Orthodox Press, 2010.

About the Author

MICHAEL WARREN DAVIS is a contributing editor for *The American Conservative* and an editor at Sophia Institute Press. He previously served as communications director for the Melkite Church in the United States, editor-in-chief of *Crisis Magazine*, and U.S. editor of the *Catholic Herald* of London. His writing has appeared in a variety of magazines from the *New York Post* to *First Things*. He invites you to follow his Substack newsletter, *Theologoumenalia*.

Sophia Institute

Sophia Institute is a nonprofit institution that seeks to nurture the spiritual, moral, and cultural life of souls and to spread the gospel of Christ in conformity with the authentic teachings of the Roman Catholic Church.

Sophia Institute Press fulfills this mission by offering translations, reprints, and new publications that afford readers a rich source of the enduring wisdom of mankind.

Sophia Institute also operates the popular online resource CatholicExchange.com. *Catholic Exchange* provides world news from a Catholic perspective as well as daily devotionals and articles that will help readers to grow in holiness and live a life consistent with the teachings of the Church.

In 2013, Sophia Institute launched Sophia Teachers to renew and rebuild Catholic culture through service to Catholic education. With the goal of nurturing the spiritual, moral, and cultural life of souls, and an abiding respect for the role and work of teachers, we strive to provide materials and programs that are at once enlightening to the mind and ennobling to the heart; faithful and complete, as well as useful and practical.

Sophia Institute gratefully recognizes the Solidarity Association for preserving and encouraging the growth of our apostolate over the course of many years. Without their generous and timely support, this book would not be in your hands.

www.SophiaInstitute.com
www.CatholicExchange.com
www.SophiaTeachers.org

Sophia Institute Press is a registered trademark of Sophia Institute.
Sophia Institute is a tax-exempt institution as defined by the
Internal Revenue Code, Section 501(c)(3). Tax ID 22-2548708.